THE
CALIFORNIA
COMMUNITY
COLLEGES

THE CALIFORNIA COMMUNITY COLLEGES

Sidney W. Brossman
Myron Roberts

Field Educational Publications, Incorporated

A Subsidiary of Field Enterprises, Incorporated

Palo Alto, Calif.   Addison, Ill.   Atlanta   Dallas   Ocean, N.J.   Portland, Oreg.

Standard Book Number 514–03041–0

CONTENTS

FOREWORD

THIS BOOK TELLS the story of California's Community Colleges, the "open door colleges," and the progress they are making toward realizing the American goal of equal opportunity in higher education. It is a book which goes beneath the rhetoric of "relevance" and other current catch-phrases to a deeper understanding of the promise and problems inherent in this effort to educate our people.

No claim is made here that the California Community Colleges have achieved perfection. But this work offers solid evidence to support the thesis that the Community Colleges are making an outstanding contribution to our society at bargain rates for the taxpayer.

I commend this book to the professional educator, the student, and the concerned citizen. For it provides essential insights into the policies and practices that have brought the Community Colleges to a position of pre-eminence in their field. And, just as important, the book points out what must be done if that position is to be maintained and strengthened in the future.

James C. Dodd
Chairman
Board of Governors of the
California Community Colleges

CHANCELLOR BROSSMAN HAS WRITTEN what may well become the definitive statement of the philosophy of California's Community Colleges. In keeping with the spirit and nature of his subject, he has managed to tell his story without the usual educational jargon which so often puzzles and exasperates the layman who sincerely wishes to understand what is happening in our colleges. Instead, he has adopted the style and techniques of the learned journalist, which he also happens to be, to delineate his ideas in a lucid, straightforward manner. This enhances the merit of the work by making it equally valuable to the professional educator and the concerned layman, as together they seek to understand and solve the problems of higher education.

Although the prime subject of this book is the California Community Colleges, I believe it will prove valuable to educators and readers throughout the nation, for the ideas and problems developed by Chancellor Brossman can easily be applied to a variety of local situations.

King Durkee
Vice Chairman
Board of Governors of the
California Community Colleges

MEMBERS OF THE BOARD OF GOVERNORS
OF THE CALIFORNIA COMMUNITY COLLEGES

PREFACE

WHY THIS BOOK...

As we approach the two hundredth anniversary of the United States of America, the nation has professed its intention to make good, perhaps somewhat belatedly, on the promise of equal opportunity for all, which was implicit in the founding of this republic. While the precise means of translating this ideal into a reality have yet to be determined, few would doubt that education, particularly higher education, must play a critical role in the achievement of this goal. For good or ill, higher education has become the portal, not only to the learned professions, but, in an increasingly scientific and technical society, to almost any job above the level of common laborer. Perhaps even more important in the long run, some degree of higher education is increasingly useful, if not absolutely required, for individuals who wish to participate fully in the social, political, cultural, and community life of the nation.

However, just as literacy was once regarded as the natural prerogative of the rich and the "wellborn," so higher education until fairly recently has tended to be restricted to the affluent. This has been generally true in America despite our democratic ideology. (In Europe, higher education has always been frankly elitist.) The problem for a democratic society has been to provide access to college for the sons and daughters of ordinary citizens and to assure readily available opportunities for self-improvement and educational growth for adults who must spend most of their days working or caring for home and children. The children of ordinary citizens are no less able to benefit from higher education than are the affluent, but they are less likely to be able to afford to travel long distances and take up residence in colleges and universities many miles from their homes. To meet this need and to provide adequate occupational education, the people in various California communities began to create, almost a century ago, two-year "post high school" educational institutions which they called "junior colleges." And the two-year colleges have provided an opportunity for people who have had to change jobs and adjust to technological changes because the economy has required them to retrain. After a slow but steady beginning, these institutions have grown with astonishing rapidity in the past two decades. Today about 850,000 people attend two-year colleges in California, about 85 percent of all students enrolled in the first two years of college in the state, including both transfer and nontransfer students. Originally a curious offshoot of higher education, this uniquely American experiment has spread from California to become a major force, not only in America but increasingly throughout the world. First other states and then country after country set out to emulate the California experience with two-year colleges in an effort to meet the "revolution of rising expectations" that is sweeping the world.

For millions of Californians, the two-year community colleges have solved the problem of access to higher education and have enabled them to enjoy not merely more rewarding employment but fuller participation in the life of the state and of the nation. For adults left jobless by a turn of the economy or by technological changes, the community colleges have provided opportunities for retraining.

The ideas and techniques that have evolved from the community college experiment in California are significant, not merely for what has already been accomplished but for the even greater impact they will have on American society in the years ahead. Thus far, the success story of the California Community Colleges remains "unwept, unhonored and unsung." The colleges have been widely emulated, but not as widely discussed, particularly in books. Therefore, this is a book which frankly focuses on the virtues and advantages of what many call "The People's Colleges."

If America is to make equal educational opportunity for all a reality rather than a slogan in the decade ahead, educators must begin to think seriously about the unique advantages and some of the problems that have grown out of California's massive experience with two-year colleges. Further, the general public needs to know more about the two-year colleges as "comprehensive campuses" where occupational education, continuing education, and academic and transfer programs exist side by side in the same institution. And the college student, present or prospective, should also know something about these institutions, whether he or she intends to go to one or not. For the fact is that many California Community Colleges have for years been practicing many of the educational innovations that students have been clamoring to introduce into the curriculum of higher education.

Finally, it should be noted that students from the various ethnic, racial, and cultural minorities—Blacks, Browns, Asians, Native Americans, and poor whites—are now going to community colleges in unprecedented numbers, and their overall success has been outstanding. Any nation agonizing over various proposals to help the educationally deprived might well look to the California Community Colleges for a conspicuous example of a program that is working.

Perhaps we should also note that the authors of this book have spent much of their professional lives working within the California Community College network and therefore count themselves among the loyal, but hopefully not uncritical, supporters of that network. Therefore, this book does not profess to present a totally objective study of the California Community Colleges, and the authors forewarn their readers that what follows is an essay stressing what we believe to be the considerable merits of these two-year colleges.

In sum, we would argue that what the village grammar school was to nineteenth-century America, what the local high school was to America in the early part of this century, the community college is becoming as we approach our third century of national life. The village grammar school was an experiment founded on what many once regarded as the absurd notion that almost any child could be made literate. The comprehensive American high school was once a no less visionary attempt to implement the ideal of a great democratic "melting pot." In an age of increasing demand for individuality, high achievement, and full citizenship for all, the community college seems the best available working model of an educational institution uniquely qualified to meet the aspirations of the great majority of Americans today.

For all of these reasons we think it is time for this book about the California Community Colleges.

S.W.B. and M.R.

THE
CALIFORNIA
COMMUNITY
COLLEGES

1

THE IDEA
OF THE
"JUNIOR COLLEGE"

A university has been defined as, ideally, "a community of scholars." With this definition as a touchstone, a California Community College could be defined as "a community of students and instructors." The difference can be illustrated by a story John Kenneth Galbraith tells of his experience while a junior member of a university economics faculty. A problem arose about the availability of certain research materials at the university library. The large numbers of students using the library often made it inconvenient for professors doing scholarly research. The faculty gathered to ponder the problem and consider possible solutions. One professor had a simple, forthright answer: Why not just issue a decree closing the library to all students?

Galbraith reports that, to his knowledge, the suggestion was not adopted. But the fact that it was put forward illustrates a certain premise about the nature and function of an institution of higher education which is relevant to an understanding of the difference between the traditional view of a university and the idea of the community college. Many early universities were often begun primarily as scholarly refuges, as academic monasteries where thoughtful and learned men might retreat from the "madding crowd" to contemplate eternal truth. Students were admitted only gradually and often with great misgivings. Innovation, particularly in subject matter, was widely regarded with both fear and contempt. Thus it was not until the last century or so that many renowned European universities condescended to permit instruction in the physical and biological sciences, since such subjects were considered merely useful and hence not honorific. The guiding spirit was that of those Greek philosophers who speculated endlessly about how many teeth are in a horse's mouth but who considered it demeaning to go and have a look. While such snobbishness and ignorance have been abandoned by most American institutions of higher education, the tradition may linger here and there. A few professors may still maintain that their primary love is research, and thus the demands of students may be subordinated to the demands of a given discipline. Although this point of view may sometimes be defensible, it could be carried to the point where the student is looked upon as an intruder, while the professor assumes the role of guardian who must stand at the gates and turn back the vulgar. In short, the idea of the university is almost inherently an elitist idea: even the founders of this democratic society, such as Thomas Jefferson, envisioned the role of higher education as limited largely to developing an aristocracy of brains and talent as

3

a substitute for an aristocracy of mere birth, as in Europe. In most four-year colleges today the primary criteria for admission of students are still academic achievement, i.e., getting good grades and scores.

The community college in California is at once both a simpler and a more complex institution. No one professes to believe that community college students are any sort of aristocracy; on the contrary, it is a matter of pride that the average student in these institutions tends to come from middle and lower socioeconomic backgrounds. A study by Edmund J. Gleazer reveals that over half of community college students hold part or full-time jobs while attending school.[1] And a large percentage are the first members of their families to attend college.

California Community College boards, elected locally and responsible directly to friends and neighbors, are not likely to forget that the college belongs to the people whose taxes support it. The typical two-year college instructor may, and often does, have a wide variety of interests outside his immediate classroom assignment, but he is not likely to be under any misapprehension as to his prime responsibility, which is, in Chaucer's simple but penetrating phrase, to "gladly teach." And, finally, the student may or may not be a scholar engaged in a search for new and profound truths or concerned with correcting the wrongs of society, but, again, he is not likely to forget that as a student his primary role is to study and learn specific subject matter toward specific ends. In this sense the community colleges are finite institutions designed to help people achieve finite goals. They are based on the simple democratic notion that education, like health, beauty, travel, and money, is a good thing and that in a democracy it ought to be available to ordinary people and to the sons and daughters of ordinary people, as well as to those who used to be called the "privileged classes."

The first two-year colleges in California began with the recognition by local townspeople that many young high school graduates who were unable to take up residence at an often distant college or university (usually for financial reasons) might benefit from college level studies. The founders of these institutions tended to be modest about their aspirations. They wanted to make it clear that they were in no sense proposing to compete with four-year universities. Hence they used the term "junior" college to describe legally the institutions they were creating. In some cases they went even further, eschewing the

---

[1]EDMUND J. GLEAZER, JR., *This Is the Community College*, Houghton Mifflin Co., 1968.

term "college" altogether in favor of such awkward designations as "two years of post high school experience," or "the thirteenth and fourteenth grades." Generally, these colleges were established by an existing high school district as just one more service offered to the community by a democratic school system. It was not long, however, before the "post high school experience" grew into full-fledged junior colleges. Ultimately these institutions became today's "comprehensive" California Community Colleges, that is, two-year colleges with academic and occupational programs on the same campus. From the very start they were highly successful, despite their uncertain status reflected by the self-consciousness about just what to call them. Large numbers of junior colleges were, for purposes of student transfer, accepted into full junior status by the four-year colleges, and, to the surprise of almost everyone, their students quickly showed that they were able to compete on an equal or better basis with students whose freshman and sophomore years had been completed at a four-year college.[2] This record of high academic performance continues to this day and has been acknowledged widely by the University of California, by the California State University and Colleges, and by such educational leaders as Clark Kerr and members of the Carnegie Commission on Higher Education.

The academic success of community college transfer student is not hard to understand if one examines the reality of the educational process. In their early stages junior colleges had been partly staffed by culling from the ranks of existing high school faculty the most experienced and successful teachers. Thus, a typical junior college freshman was likely to find himself in a relatively small class led by a mature teacher who had distinguished himself sufficiently to be chosen for what amounted to a promotion. The teacher, on the other hand, accustomed to meeting classes 25 to 30 hours a week in the high school, was apt to regard his 15- to 21-hour teaching load at the college level as a great blessing, enabling him to spend far more time preparing for classes, counseling students and reading students' papers. These inherent advantages of the junior college compensated for, and in many cases outweighed, some of the disadvantages of more provincial campuses, smaller libraries, and fewer eminent scholars on the faculty.

Thus the designation "junior college" was, in the strict sense of

---

[2]LELAND L. MEDSKER and DALE TILLERY, *Breaking the Access Barriers*, McGraw-Hill, 1971. This work cites several studies which document the success of community college transfer students at four-year institutions.

ordinary English, a misnomer. For what the new colleges offered was not a democratic version of the English "prep school," which is what the title suggests; in fact, junior college courses were compatible with the same courses being offered at four-year colleges.

Still, the "junior college" label stuck for a long period. The label persisted partly because a name, once adopted, is hard to shake; partly because of the modesty of some local school boards, administrators, and faculty members; and perhaps partly because of an attitude that sometimes eschewed the intellectual pretensions associated with words like "college" and "professor." (Some two-year college instructors still decline to use the title "professor" or a system of academic rank for faculty members.)

Once into the "post high school education" syndrome, however, two-year colleges quickly found themselves moving into new and unanticipated fields. Like the land-grant colleges established by Congress in the nineteenth century to facilitate the training of farmers, school teachers, and ministers, and which grew into the state colleges and universities of today, the two-year colleges found themselves being asked to provide a variety of educational services. Business and professional men in the community were quick to see these institutions as a source of skilled technicians and semiprofessional employees. Occupational and business programs began to flourish. California's rapid industrial growth required an almost limitless supply of electronics technicians, skilled salesmen, mechanics, secretaries, and data-processing technicians—people who had some specialized knowledge beyond that commonly taught in the high schools, but less training than that of the full-fledged graduate engineer or accountant, for example. Occupational training programs were generally so successful that college administrators found themselves facing a problem—not with placing their occupational graduates in a job—but with keeping people in the program until their education had been completed, because many firms were willing to hire these people just as quickly as they had grasped the barest fundamentals.

World War II, and then the Korean and Vietnam wars, added still another element to the growth of the two-year colleges.[3] Veterans, often with families, were anxious to use their educational benefits to obtain a degree as quickly, economically, and efficiently as possible. Many of them were disinclined to use their slender resources in

---

[3]MEDSKER and TILLERY, *Breaking the Access Barriers.*

"name" institutions, particularly for the first two years. Many went to community colleges and, by and large, were so successful that the GI Bill has become accepted universally as an outstanding example of a federal government program that works.

Finally, another significant development in the role of the community colleges, largely unanticipated by the founders of the two-year colleges, was the extremely large number of adults who came to these institutions. Large numbers of adults, began to flock to two-year college classes—day and night. Some of these were "late bloomers"—people in their twenties and thirties, many of whom had previously given up on education. People who had quit school, got married, or gone to work started showing up. They ranged from 20 to 80 years of age. They returned to school for retraining, for technological training, and for all sorts of other reasons. And they had one thing in common: a desire to learn. Thus, the California Community Colleges became places where those who, for whatever reason, had previously failed to take full advantage of the public school system had an opportunity to try once again.

In a typical California Community College classroom today one might find a policeman seeking to further his professional career through higher education sitting beside an ex-convict working for the federal government rehabilitating young drug users; a woman who holds a degree in music but has returned to college to study nursing; a salesman who wants to be a lawyer; a steelworker who wants to study economics; an ambulance attendant who seeks to become an M.D.; and innumerable young housewives who wish to enter a trade or profession as their children grow older and less dependent. Some of these people will fail; many will not. There is hardly a profession or institution of any size or scope in California that does not have among its most valued members people who began their reeducation under similar circumstances. There are innumerable doctors, lawyers, legislators, college instructors, engineers, scientists, and business leaders working in California today who took a gamble on a second chance at higher education and won.

One reason for the relatively swift acceptance of the community college in California by the leaders of the state's traditional four-year colleges and universities was that it became clear that these new institutions were providing a valuable "screening" service for the four-year colleges. In a state like California, where upward mobility is highly valued, the demand for access to higher education was so great as to constitute a virtually irresistible political force. The community colleges often provided a happy alternative to lowering traditionally high standards for admission to other institutions.

Typically, only about one in every three students who enrolled at a community college with the professed intention of transferring to a four-year institution actually did so. Thus it was probably implicit in the community college experiment that, along with an academic program preparing students for transfer to four-year institutions, there would have to be extensive education for a variety of occupational and technical programs where people with something less than a full four-year college degree were needed. Such programs have been so successful and have grown so rapidly that today students enrolled in occupational and vocational programs (that is, programs which can be completed on one campus, which may vary in length from a few weeks to over two years, and which culminate in something other than the traditional bachelor's degree) now constitute a majority of students on many community college campuses.

The decision in 1967 by the state legislature and Governor Ronald Reagan to authorize a statewide Board of Governors of the California Community Colleges and thereby change the official designation of the state's network of two-year campuses from "junior college" to "community college" reflected official cognizance of the fact that the tentative, local, and experimental phase had ended and that these institutions had indeed become an indispensable element in the state's overall program for public higher education. (This legislation was authored by Senator Walter Stiern of Bakersfield.) The years of continuing growth and progress under the leadership of the Board of Governors have reaffirmed this fact.

Today, the California Community Colleges are providing a number of unique and invaluable education services, many of which will be detailed in this book. But in a broad and general way the two-year colleges differ from their four-year counterparts in California in the following:

1. The community colleges offer the least expensive access to higher education available in the state to the general public. The importance of this fact cannot be exaggerated. By making higher education available at a reputable, tuition-free, neighborhood college, the state and the community reaffirm this nation's highest tradition of faith in the individual's ability to better himself through his own efforts.

2. The community colleges uniquely offer both academic and occupational programs on the same campus (thus, the "comprehensive col-

lege"), permitting the student to move easily from one to the other without artificial and arbitrary distinctions and distractions.

3. The community colleges are required by law to admit any high school graduate and may enroll any student who has reached the age of 18. This fact is in itself perhaps one of the most sweeping advances achieved for the cause of education since the advent of the first compulsory public school. At the same time the success of community college graduates, both in the classroom and on the job, demolishes many of the classic presumptions supporting traditional ideas about higher education.

4. Community colleges offer extensive counseling and guidance programs. Their freshmen and sophomores can expect to receive a great deal of personal attention.

5. The community colleges have proven uniquely suited to meeting the educational needs of minority-group students in terms both of numbers of such students enrolled and of success achieved in the classroom.

6. Alone among the three segments of public higher education in California, two-year colleges are governed by local boards elected by the people. They are staffed by instructors and administrators directly responsible to the communities they serve.

7. Community colleges are primarily teaching institutions; that is their reason for existence.

American society presumes that people ought to care about themselves and try to improve the quality of their lives. The two-year colleges provide an educational opportunity for many who could not otherwise attend an institution of higher education. The practical experience of the California Community Colleges, the hard-won successes of their students, the diligence and creativity of their faculties, and the devotion of their administrators and trustees have demolished both the misnomer "junior college" and the myth of educational inferiority which surrounded it.

2

WHO SHOULD GO TO COLLEGE? WHAT'S A COLLEGE FOR?

Whatever the names we give to colleges, there has, ironically, never been a time in American history when the demands for higher education were greater or the benefits less certain. When only a small percentage of the total number of young people were able to attend, the advantages inherent in a higher education were self-evident. First of all, colleges were the portal through which one simply had to pass in order to gain entry to the learned professions and, to a considerable extent, prestigious, highly paid employment. But perhaps even more important to the majority of students, a college education provided certain social advantages that led almost inevitably to concomitant economic gains. Despite America's professed democratic disdain for intellectual snobbery and our official admiration for the man who lifts himself by his own bootstraps, the managerial class of our principal industries and institutions has been dominated, in practice, by college-trained people.

And then college education was supposed to give a man or woman "a certain polish," an appreciation for "the finer things of life"—all of which translated into an ability to master the style, the idiom, and the outlook of the cultured elite.

Today we are far less certain of the validity of almost all these generalizations than people were fifty years ago. We are no longer even sure what constitutes a learned profession. Medicine and law and the exact sciences retain something of their old mystique. But what of the army of accountants, engineers, teachers, nurses, technicians, and business administrators turned out by our colleges every year? Are they members of a learned profession or simply people who have acquired a high degree of knowledge and skill qualifying them to do a certain job competently?

As to the social benefits of higher education, perhaps a glance at what has happened to men's fashions will provide us with some insight into that question. A decade or so ago it was common for young men who wanted to look "sharp" and fashionable to cultivate an "Ivy League" look. It was assumed that the students in our most socially prestigious eastern universities were the natural trend-setters in fashion. Now the young men in the Ivy League colleges, and in most other colleges throughout the nation, seem to prefer *The Grapes of Wrath* look. What is true of fashions is true of a great many other areas of life: the idea of the "natural" social leadership of the educated elite just is not given much credence any more. A brilliant undergraduate student at Harvard, for example, can no longer look forward—almost as a matter of course—to taking his ultimate place in the U.S. Senate or on the Supreme Court or as the chairman of the board of a large corporation. He may find himself passed over in favor of a former brilliant young student from one of the California Community Colleges. This is happening now to some extent, as a matter of fact, and it seems reasonable to believe that it will be even more prevalent a decade or two hence when today's undergraduates begin to compete for top positions in society.

The economic recession of the late 1960s and early 1970s taught a good many people some hard lessons about education—and prompted a widespread reexamination of the functions, objectives, and nature of higher education. The demand for engineers and teachers was thought to be virtually limitless; thousands of young people confidently enrolled in college in the firm expectation that graduation day would bring plenty of choices among attractive alternatives. Instead we saw the depression-like specter of college graduates unable to find any kind of suitable work. Often they were denied even unskilled jobs that went to the less educated because, "You wouldn't be happy doing that kind of work."

Further, the larger society, feeling the increasing squeeze of higher taxes and somewhat disenchanted by the behavior of a minority of students and faculty members, changed its attitude toward higher education. Put off by a value system among some students that appeared to regard rock musicians and street poets more highly than business and industrial leaders, our society became clearly less enthusiastic and more critical in its support for colleges than was the case a few years before. Finally, the flood of migration to California slowed considerably.

As a consequence, enrollment at some four-year institutions levelled off sharply in California, and some plans for building additional campuses to accommodate an anticipated onrush of students were scrapped. The community colleges continued to grow, although somewhat less rapidly than a few years earlier.

What seems to be happening is a reevaluation of an idea almost everyone accepted in the late fifties and early sixties: the idea that every young person should go to college. The belief that education, like health, is an absolute good, and the more of it people have the better for them and for the entire community, is no longer as widely accepted in America, even by educators, as it once was. Today, a good many educators who have studied and thought about the future of higher education in the United States would be more apt to assert:

"Probably *almost* everyone should go to college, and the majority of those who do should attend two-year community colleges."

For example, the Carnegie Commission on Higher Education, perhaps the nation's single most distinguished body of men and women providing independent and yet authoritative review of the problems of higher education, proposes that by 1980 from 35 to 40 percent of all undergraduate education in the United States be accomplished by community colleges and urges the establishment of a minimum of 230 to 280 new colleges by 1980 to accomplish this goal.

In the Commission's words: "The community college has proved its great worth to American society. Community colleges should be available, within commuting distance, to all persons throughout their lives, except in sparsely settled areas...."[1]

The Commission goes on to hail the community colleges as "The most striking recent structural development in higher education in the United States." And it proceeds to give the reasons for their rapid growth. This is worth quoting, since it goes to the heart of the question of who should go to college, specifically to a community college.

Among the explanations for the rapid advance of the community colleges are their open-admission policies, their geographic distribution in many states and their usually low tuition policies. They offer more varied programs for a greater variety of students than any other segment of higher education. They provide a chance for many who are not fully committed in advance to a four-year college career to try out higher education without great risk of time or money. They appeal to students who are undecided about their future careers and unprepared to choose a field of specialization. And, last but by no means least, they provide an opportunity for continuing education to working adults seeking to upgrade their skills and training.[2]

Perhaps the key sentence in this statement is the reference to the variety of programs, and hence of students, to be found in the community colleges. The variety reflects the goal of democratic pluralism at its highest and best. Thus, the California Community Colleges offer over 3,200 separate occupational education programs, most of them of one or two years' duration. At the same time, in some of the state's two-year colleges as many as 40 percent of the students

---

[1]MEDSKER and TILLERY, *Breaking the Access Barrier.*

[2]MEDSKER and TILLERY, *Breaking the Access Barrier.*

were fully eligible for admission to the University of California or the California State University and Colleges when they elected to enroll in a two-year institution as freshmen because of economy, convenience, or other reasons. Not a few do so because they are convinced they will receive an education more suited to their needs.

Until fairly recently the majority of students entered a two-year college with the announced intention of transferring to a four-year institution and ultimately graduating with a baccalaureate degree. A great many of these succeed brilliantly. Some do not. They drop out to go to work or to get married or they switch to a vocational training program. Here the phrase "drop out" may be misleading, for it may suggest failure. From society's point of view, as well as the student's, however, a decision to leave a program leading to a degree in engineering in favor of taking a job as a technician may well represent success rather than failure. In effect, the two-year college has "screened" the would-be engineer, not on the basis of previous grades or performance on an aptitude test, neither of which always corresponds with success on the job, but by trial and error. Assuming that a student could have enrolled in a four-year institution, the subsequent savings to the taxpayers becomes very great indeed. For the individual, too, there is an equivalent savings in time and money, as the Carnegie Commission has noted. This is not to say that there may not be significant attrition in two-year colleges. Some students who should have stayed to complete a program may drop out. (This is a situation for which community colleges are seeking appropriate solutions.)

It should be pointed out that the guidance function in the community colleges is given a role commensurate with classroom instruction. Counselors are available and accessible, and most are specialists in one phase or another of the complex problems of helping people plan their futures and set realistic goals for themselves. Thus many potential "dropouts" are saved by counselors skilled in pointing up alternatives. Others are sometimes told, quite frankly, that they might best spend their time acquiring work experience, applying for government service of one kind or another, or pursuing other nonacademic activities, perhaps with the intention of resuming their academic instruction or training at some later date.

However, saying that perhaps not everyone should go to college is quite different from saying that certain kinds of people should not be permitted to try. The glory of two-year public higher education in California is precisely the fact that—like the Mother Church of the Middle Ages—its doors are open to everyone, including educational sinners sincerely seeking redemption. The community colleges have thousands of students who did not do well in high school but who are achieving well now that they have a few years of maturity to sharpen their sense of educational purpose. On each campus in the state there are ex-dropouts earning good grades, and there are others from the depths of society learning not only to become useful members of society but leaders in their own communities—raw, aimless, and confused young people who seem suddenly to become transformed into serious and purposeful adults.

Saving lost or wayward souls is, quite frankly, an essential element in the two-year college educational mission. Obviously, even a minimal restriction of the open-admissions policy would eliminate a great many of these persons. The essential factor is that the student who comes to the community college should feel the need to try to learn the subject he has come to study, or master whatever program he has embarked upon. And since there appears to be no way that the state can, as a matter of law, distinguish in advance between those who will try and those who will not, open admissions should be continued.

No question is more fundamental to a democratic society than the matter of access. The Declaration of Independence guarantees Americans "Life, Liberty, and the Pursuit of Happiness." We think the Declaration means not only liberty from, but liberty *to*. The right to try, to compete, to excel is inherent in the American system. The open, beckoning, raw land of the West was once the concrete embodiment and symbol of that promise. Today fences have gone up around most of the great institutions of our society. The schoolroom has replaced the prairie as the symbol of opportunity.

Access to wealth, to power, and to knowledge underlie half the great domestic issues of our day. Much of the public discussion of this question tends to focus on the poor and disadvantaged and all those who, in one way or another, have been denied full and equal opportunity and participation. This is proper and necessary. In addition, there is another case for equal access.

The genius of American society is precisely that it has found means and created institutions that make it possible to use those human resources that some other societies have wasted and ignored. Our preeminence in industrial development, for example, has been largely the work of poor and obscure young migrants and sons of migrants who—had they not come to America—would probably have lived and died poor and obscure: men like Edison, Carnegie, Ford. How many Einsteins lived out their lives in the ghettos of Europe without ever having been introduced to the mysteries of mathematics? How many "mute inglorious Miltons" lie buried and forgotten because they were never taught to read?

A major premise that underlies the community college experiment in California is that there reside in every human community certain talents, potential abilities, and capacities which—given guidance, training, and disciplined knowledge—can be put to work for the benefit not only of the individual, but also of the entire community. In fact, the premise is no longer only a premise; it is a demonstrable truth. And the experiment is no longer merely experimental. It works.

Californians alone produce more wealth annually than all but a relatively few nations in the world. What was only a century ago a land of arid deserts and forbidding mountains today has one of the highest per capita incomes in the world. California's tax-supported public system of higher education has played a major role in bringing this miracle to pass.

In the present global struggle to maintain our position of economic preeminence, the 96 California Community Colleges constitute an immense asset. For their existence means that in virtually every populated area of the state, people who wish to learn may draw upon the skill, experience, and insights of accomplished instructors and excellent facilities to help them achieve their personal objectives. Almost no one is excluded. And thus, as these words are written, hundreds of thousands of Californians who understand that knowledge is power, that in fact it may be the *only* really lasting kind of power, are using these resources to change themselves and hence their society for the better.

Who, then, should go particularly to a community college?

First of all, people, young and old, of exceptional abilities who seek to achieve some extraordinary goal. The high school graduate, for example, who is accustomed to winning high academic honors and enjoys the game of ideas, may find a community college a more accessible and responsive theater for his talents than a large university. Teaching the 18- and 19-year-old freshman and sophomore is a prime responsibility of community colleges. The same group may necessarily take a subordinate role to upperclassmen and graduate students at some large universities. A freshman with something original and interesting to say will likely find classmates and faculty members who will listen and challenge him at a community college. His individual talents will likely be recognized and encouraged, his shortcomings noted and pointed out. Community college faculty, like most faculties throughout all segments of higher education, has no responsibility more important than its students.

Second, students should go to a community college if they simply wish to go to school to acquire a marketable skill and learn something about themselves and the society they live in: that is, the great majority of college students. Such students usually find the transition from high school to college life easier and more graceful, less subject to what some have called academic culture shock. Thus most people will find the community college not merely accessible and inexpensive, but also a shade more appropriate for them, which is probably why the great majority of all college students may choose within the next decade to go to these institutions, not merely in California but throughout the nation.

Third, persons of every age who wish to learn more about a specific subject, skill, or vocation should make use of their local two-year college. The point need not be labored, since the California Community Colleges offer programs of such great size and diversity, and since we live in a technological society, the implications of this are obvious.

In the words of one young man, now pursuing a California Community College computer programming course, "I spent five years as a welder until automation came along and cost me my job. I decided I'd better be one of the people who learns to run the machine or else the machine will run my life."

Finally, a word about one of the most important and least discussed groups within the community college student body: the "older folks"—from 30 to 80—who return to school. Over the years the average age of the community college student has been creeping up. It is now in the mid-twenties. While many students are still 18-, 19-, and 20-year-olds, the proportion of mature students has been rising steadily. Enormous numbers of Californians are deciding somewhere in the middle years to embrace entirely new professions. Housewives or unskilled or semiskilled workers decide to become teachers, lawyers, or accountants. A surprising number of them succeed. (Indeed, the younger students have come to complain about unfair competition from the older folks, who often take a highly serious view of their educational commitment, and who, paradoxically, although they are busier than the young people, have more time to study.)

Apart from those with grand, long-term objectives in mind, there are substantial numbers of mature students who wish simply to pursue specific courses to meet a problem or enhance their earning ability. For example, many graduates in such fields as business or one of the sciences enroll in freshman literature courses simply because they are interested in reading and writing. At Chaffey College a judge has enrolled in Spanish courses so he can communicate better with persons who speak little or no English.

The mature student represents one of the most refreshing and valued elements in the total educational experience at the community colleges. By and large, more older people may wish to take advantage of the institutions they help to pay for. This is particularly true of those who would like to attend but are afraid to try because they might be "too old" or "unable to compete with those kids." Most successful community college adults admit they had these fears before enrolling and laugh at them later.

Ignorance is a kind of prison. Education is the means by which we seek to escape the limits of time, circumstances, and all else that confines us. Educators have debated the aims of education for many years without unanimity of agreement.

Nevertheless people try—as indeed they should. It has been argued that the function of education is to transmit the culture and heritage of a given society; to enlighten the soul to The True, The Beautiful, and The Good; to serve as a critic of a culture and its values; to save civilization from an ecological or nuclear Armageddon; or to help earn a living. Each of these points of view has its champions and its own inner logic. Such champions may be found on virtually every California Community College campus. But, generally speaking, the two-year colleges, born as a practical response to specific human and social needs, tend to have an eclectic approach toward such questions.

The pragmatism that characterizes the community college approach to education tends, inevitably, to give these institutions a bias in the direction of occupationalism. However, the term "occupation" should be understood both in its broadest and in its more specific implications—that is, in the sense of people discovering what to do with their lives as well as learning how to earn a living. Thus, Ortega y Gassett speaks of every youth having to discover his true vocation in life before becoming a fully mature human being. In that sense the community colleges are primarily occupationally oriented.

Thus a young person often comes to his local community college after graduating from high school with no sharply defined vocational goal in mind. Vaguely, he feels a need for "a college education." He is under no great economic pressure to work full-time, since he is still living at home, and the convenience and low cost of his neighborhood college make it possible for him to meet most or all of both his college and personal expenses with a part-time job. Usually his parents want him to continue his education and, if possible or necessary, will help him to that end. In his first year he takes a variety of courses and quickly discovers that there is after all a difference between high school and college. He is on his own to a far greater extent in respect to classroom attendance, meeting assignments, and other academic chores. Instructors and counselors will help him, but normally he will be encouraged to seek their help rather than having it thrust inappropriately upon him. The assumption is that he is a mature human being.

With a little luck and a reasonable supply of normal curiosity and idealism he is likely to find, somewhere in that first year or so of general education, an instructor or a subject that captures his interest and engages his imagination. Chances are that if he likes a certain subject, he will be successful at it. Success will stimulate him to further effort and commitment. He will begin to see not only a job but a way of life, an adult role in society, built around his interest.

His other courses now may begin to fall into place and take on a meaning they had lacked before insofar as they contribute toward his new-found goal. If he persists, he is well on the path toward maturity, as Ortega y Gassett has defined it: that is, having a sense of purpose, being "in charge" of one's own destiny, and having the ability "to make a stand within oneself."

To take another example, a friend of ours, a middle-aged businessman, has retired from the newspaper business to write books. In addition to writing books, he is interested in two fields, broadcast journalism and real estate investment. He plans to finance his writing by investing his savings in California real estate. He is interested in broadcasting because of a long desire to perform on camera. Therefore he has enrolled in two courses at his local community college, one in broadcasting, the other in real estate. This is an example of a relatively specific and narrow use that one individual finds for his local college.

Whether the subject is welding, philosophy, real estate, law, nursing, or remedial English, the community colleges exist to help people learn more about subjects as varied as the community itself. Generally speaking, the colleges have avoided efforts to establish a hierarchy of values with respect to subject matter, students, or faculty. Those who teach vocational courses are paid the same number of dollars and hold the same academic rank as those who teach other courses, given equal training and experience. This offends some people who feel that there are "noble" and "worthy" subjects and "ignoble" subjects. Most community colleges tend to act on the assumption that discussion about what is "higher" knowledge and what is "lower" knowledge has about as much validity today as the question of how many angels could dance on the head of a pin, which was supposed to have preoccupied medieval philosophers.

We have written thus far largely of the contributions community colleges make to individuals in pursuit of their private objectives. But a tax-supported institution clearly has a social role as well. There is no need here to belabor the critical importance of education, at all levels, to the success and stability of any modern industrial nation. The community colleges are unique, however, in that they are providing higher education for enormous numbers of people who have traditionally been outside the framework of college education. Apart from their specific vocational pursuit, students are exposed to knowledge, insight, and awareness in fields such as history, philosophy, psychology, and sociology that go far deeper than is possible in a typical high school course. The benefits to society are immense. For in every town or city in the nation where these institutions exist, every year thousands upon thousands of people are crossing an invisible but very real line that once separated the "college man" from the ordinary citizen. There are already several communities in California where the average citizen now has the equivalent of at least one year of college education. In the near future this will probably become the norm for most communities in California.

The community colleges exist to provide a relatively convenient, inexpensive way for those who desire training, wisdom, insight, understanding, and specific skills in a variety of socially worthwhile activities and subjects with the help and guidance of those who already have demonstrated some degree of mastery in the field. In the long run the community colleges may or may not help to redeem mankind or save civilization. But in the short run they take a considerable satisfaction in doing something useful.

3

THE POOR AND THE COMMUNITY COLLEGE

Education may not be a cure-all for social ills, but it is often the midwife of affluence.

It has been said that whereas society once existed at the expense of the poor, the poor now exist at the expense of society. This remark may be somewhat of an exaggeration, but the generalization does contain an important truth about a significant change that has occurred in how society thinks about the poor and how the poor now think about society. Until fairly recently, most Americans accepted the idea that a certain amount of poverty, even extreme poverty, was an inevitable consequence of a free economy. Competition and winning have always been very important values to Americans, and if there were to be winners, it followed that there must be losers. The label or, if you prefer, the rationalization, often affixed to this simple yet basic idea was social Darwinism, because in effect it justified poverty by applying the Darwinian notion of survival of the fittest to the marketplace. In practice, of course, social Darwinism was often mitigated by private charity—the Judeo-Christian ethic preached that the rich had an obligation to the widow, the orphan, the sick, and all those "good poor" who presumably simply couldn't help themselves. Also, it should be noted that as long ago as 1597 England had its "poor laws"—in effect, a minimal welfare program designed to prevent actual starvation.

Implicit in this notion was the belief that the "good poor"—now often called the "working poor"—served a vital function in society. As the song said, "Someone had to tote the cotton," pick the fruit, do the dull, mindless factory jobs, haul away the garbage, and do all the other chores indispensable to the creation of those comforts that provided the material basis for middle- and upper-class life and leisure.

But the introduction of machinery and various labor-saving devices has profoundly altered this situation. Machines replaced millions of the working poor, in effect forcing them to give up their traditional way of life and choose between fighting their way into the middle class—which usually meant acquiring an education or some form of skilled training—or becoming more or less permanent charity cases. A major motivation behind the migration of millions of Blacks from the rural South to the cities of the North and the West, for example, was prompted by the fact that their labor was no longer required in the fields.

Social Darwinism gradually gave way to another concept: the welfare state. Fostered in this country by the New Deal and subsequent conservative as well as liberal administrations, the notion was widely accepted that the poor were simply a more or less inevitable burden on society—like a standing army—that must, in effect, be shouldered by the more affluent. But welfare, while meeting the minimal physical needs of the indigent, has proven a profoundly unpopular and in the long run perhaps unworkable method of dealing with the problems posed by the poor. Poor people have resented the paternalism of a society that in effect gives them a check once a month and asks them to cause no trouble. Middle class people have hotly resented the necessity of paying steadily ascending tax bills in order to subsidize the lives of an ever-growing army of their seemingly idle fellow citizens. In effect, many argue, the competitive system is being subverted so that the winners, instead of being rewarded, are being penalized by having to pay for the losers.

It is obvious to any thoughtful observer of the contemporary American scene that we stand at the portal of some fundamentally new approach to this problem. The present welfare system is roundly condemned by many, including many of its direct beneficiaries, as wasteful and degrading. Our concern here is with the role of the community colleges in helping to meet this problem.

Clearly, the poor no longer represent even a potential asset to society in the sense of a ready reservoir of available cheap labor. The fact that millions of Californians are on welfare is no help to a grower who needs a large supply of temporary, unskilled labor. In a sense, it is a hindrance, for the potential worker must in effect choose between the job and welfare payments, and the purely economic differences are often very marginal. Apart from welfare payments, the poor are a drain upon society in that economically depressed areas are almost always high crime areas, resulting in large police forces, crowded courts, and a profound sense of anxiety in the more affluent sections of the community. Also, the chronic poor are often tempted to look for shortcuts as a means of escaping their condition: the plague of drug abuse that rages in almost every American community is said to have begun in the nation's most poverty-stricken slums.

For all these reasons and many more that could be put forward, and leaving aside any question of humanitarian or idealistic motives, society is coming to recognize that poverty is a curse, not just for the poor, but for the entire community.

In one form or another, education is one indispensable tool for breaking the cycle of poverty and dependence. Many of the California

Community Colleges have, of course, understood and acted upon this premise for many years.

From the start of its activity in 1968, the Board of Governors of the California Community Colleges put the issue of greater opportunities for disadvantaged students as one of its very top priorities. And the record of the Board of Governors in this endeavor is at least one of the best of any statewide board anywhere.

One of the early actions of the Board of Governors was to declare its intent to examine the plight of community college students who are poor and handicapped by reason of cultural, social, and educational background—and then to do something about it. The board added its voice and considerable strength to the work of community college campuses and organizations in developing the rationale and evidence to convince state government to provide assistance to economically deprived students, and to recruit such potential students who otherwise would not have an opportunity to attend college.

Thus in 1969 the state formally charged the Board of Governors of the California Community Colleges with the responsibility of administering a program aimed at providing specific grants, aid, and services to students from low-income families. Extended Opportunity Programs and Services (EOPS), operated at the local level by the community colleges and funded by the state along with varying funding at the local level, includes a wide variety of services, ranging from direct financial aid to students, to on-the-job training, tutoring, counseling, and book loans. At Merced College, for example, the college has rebated to employers of minority students 70 percent of their salary for a six-month period of on-the-job training. Under this plan students worked 30 hours a week while carrying 12 units of college work. Employers agreed that, if satisfied with the work of their trainees, they would hire them on a permanent basis.

Still commonly called "SB 164" for its Senate Bill designation and authored by Senator Alfred E. Alquist of San Jose, the bill originally included an annual appropriation of $10 million for grants and educational services for disadvantaged students in community colleges. Adopted late in the year, the act was funded with $3 million. Although funding for EOPS has had its ups and downs ($3 to $4.5 million and $3.35 to $4.85 million), the program itself has been highly successful. Of this latter amount, about 66 percent of the funds are used for financial aid, 30 percent for educational aid, and only 4 percent for administration. Starting with 46 projects in 44 community colleges, the program currently funds 84 projects in 88 community colleges, and is responsible for grants and educational services for approximately 21,200 students. When this number is added to an estimated 40,000 students receiving assistance in one form or another, primarily funded through federal programs, the totals begin to become large enough to make a significant difference, even in a time when many useful programs were cut or eliminated because of tight budgetary considerations.

A remarkable feature of EOPS is the extent to which it has generated additional funds expended at the local level. Not only have local boards of trustees greatly increased their budget expenditures for EOPS, but surrounding communities, fraternal and business organizations, faculty, and students have also donated sizable amounts to campus programs. Early doubts about EOPS, at both the community and state levels, melted away as the program turned out to be one of the most successful experiments, economically and socially, in the history of higher education in the state and, indeed, the nation.

The California Community Colleges borrowed ideas from each other, profited from their mistakes, and developed in-service training for faculty and administration participation in the program. The Board of Governors sponsored workshops throughout the state to share methods and solutions to emerging problems. And early skeptics began to see that this was one of the best investments ever made by the California taxpayer—an investment in human capital to make productive citizens from those who might otherwise never have had a chance.

Everyone associated with EOPS took it so seriously and worked so hard at it—with a sense of personal commitment and trust—that the reputation of the program became enviable and impressive. Donations of time and money rather than bureaucratic inefficiency and waste became the hallmarks of the program.

Perhaps no previous program in the California Community Colleges has ever been more dissected and evaluated than EOPS. Allocations of dollars and evaluations of performance were scrutinized and discussed in depth in public meetings and hearings. Administrative Code regulations were developed and revised by the Board of Governors, and examinations and investigations were conducted by outside agencies and groups and then evaluated by other task forces and teams. In addition, an Advisory Committee on Extended Programs and Services, appointed by the state legislature and the Board of Governors, provides recommendations for this program.

Despite the lack of funds available and many unmet needs,

despite the newness of the program and the relative inexperience of many administering it, EOPS in the community colleges has stood up remarkably well. Over 68,000 students have been helped so far by this program. Many have been able to go on to four-year institutions; others have been able to get immediate employment as trained technicians and skilled employees. Many would not have attended a college at all had it not been for this program.

But many other advantages have come to the California Community Colleges as a result of EOPS. Techniques developed in the programs, such as peer counseling, innovative teaching practices, and many others, are now being used in regular programs. Ties between community colleges and their communities have been strengthened, and the reputation of these institutions as leaders in higher education that care about the underprivileged has been enhanced throughout the state and the nation.

Not only would many students not have been able to attend college without grants for transportation, books, and subsistence, but the colleges themselves would not have been able to foot the entire bill for special educational services and for counseling designed specifically for the needs of poor students whose backgrounds had trapped them and threatened to inhibit any chances for further educational development and training.

EOPS in the community colleges has been a model for other higher education institutions and other states. It is a common occurrence for colleges and universities in and out of the state to call upon the California Community Colleges for advice and consultation about EOPS programs.

The community colleges, however, did not rest on their laurels, nor did they stop with the development of one of the nation's model EOPS programs. All elements of the community college family— trustees, students, faculty, and administrators—again united in developing legislation for the College Opportunity Grant (COG) program, through which California now provides grants to needy college students. The COG program has been administered by the State Scholarship and Loan Commission primarily for disadvantaged students in the community colleges and for students in other segments of higher education.

A major plank in the policy of the Board of Governors to assist disadvantaged students has been to give special attention to opportunities for ethnic and racial minorities—Blacks, Browns, Asians, Native Americans—in the community colleges. (And the concern has not been limited to minority students, but extended to recruitment of minority faculty and administrators on campuses and staff members in the state Chancellor's Office.) One of the early actions of the Board of Governors was to adopt a model affirmative action program for the California Community Colleges and to urge local boards to adopt similar programs. Many had already done so, and many more subsequently developed and adopted such programs with the help of community leaders in their areas.

Community colleges have faced the issue of discrimination against minorities squarely and positively. All 96 of these institutions were asked by the Board of Governors to develop equal opportunity clauses in outside contracts to insure that the percentage of minorities hired by contractors is consistent with the proportion of minorities in those respective communities. On-the-job training opportunities were set up for minorities, and examinations were made of every aspect of college life to insure equal and fair participation of minority groups.

The Board of Governors established special credentials designed for instruction of Mexican-American and Afro-American studies. And the board, while eliminating all state Administrative Code requirements for specific courses needed for graduation, required each community college in the state to offer a course in ethnic studies as a part of the general education program.

But perhaps the greatest effort of the Board of Governors on behalf of minorities was in respect to increasing the number of minority students on community college campuses and minority staff in community colleges and in the Chancellor's Office. Results were swift and gratifying. In 1970 day enrollments increased 12 percent over 1969, but in contrast minority enrollment increased 20.5 percent, up to 21.9 percent of the total. Minority faculty and staff in 1970 were 12.5 percent, a 48 percent increase over 1967. Since 1967, total community college staff increased 38 percent, but minority employment in community colleges increased 123 percent. All minority percentages increased among the staffs of the community colleges: 7.6 percent administration, up from 1.8 percent in 1967; 8.6 percent faculty, up from 5.2 percent; and 21.1 percent other employees, up from 14.5 percent. More recently minority percentages have gone still higher, including 9 percent administration, 9.5 percent faculty, 22 percent other employees, and 23 percent in the state Chancellor's Office.

While continuing with these efforts, the California Community

Colleges are also engaged in eliminating discrimination against minorities in apprenticeship programs. Steps are now being taken to insure equal opportunity in apprenticeship programs; sponsors are required to develop affirmative action plans. Steps are also being taken to permit community colleges to be involved in the recruitment and selection of students who enter apprenticeship programs. In addition, community colleges sought and received the participation of minority groups on accreditation teams to evaluate efforts in providing equal opportunity in hiring at all levels. And as the last of the non-district territories in the state begin to align themselves with community college districts, there is also legislation to insure that the issue of adequate accessibility for minority groups will be considered as one of the criteria for alignment.

Much more needs to be done, but community colleges have demonstrated their commitment to and belief in the necessity for searching out all the many students who need special help, students who would not otherwise be going to college, and any of our citizens who have been neglected and forgotten in the educational processes of our society.

The initial success of EOPS is affirmed by a number of objective factors. The number of community colleges desiring to participate has increased sharply. Students enrolled under the EOPS program have done very well. The wide-ranging appeal of the program is also attested to by the racial and ethnic mixture of those who have taken advantage of it: roughly, 30 percent Black, 30 percent Mexican-American, 30 percent Caucasian, and 10 percent Asian-American, American Indian, and other nonwhite groups.

College administrators and faculty report that the initial impact of EOPS on campus has been a success, not only in terms of assistance to those who need it, but also in the contribution made to the general style and tone of the campus. The process of cross-culturalization has been speeded up, and innovations stemming from EOPS have in many cases provided a stimulus to new and different approaches to the regular college programs and in counseling and tutoring. A ready analogy can be made with the experience of many American colleges teaching the flood of veterans who descended on the campus after World War II. The GI Bill sent millions of young Americans to college who might otherwise never have been able to afford higher education. The result proved a boon, not only to the veterans who were the direct beneficiaries, but also to the colleges, which almost invariably reported that the veterans were better, more mature, and more serious students than those who had customarily attended college prior to World War II. Indeed, the appearance of the veterans on campus in great numbers was probably the beginning of the end of the "Joe College" syndrome in American education. The nation's universities never quite recovered from the impact of all those students who frankly wanted an education and who did not regard football and dating and joining fraternities as the most important activities on campus. The infusion of poor and minority students into higher education, hitherto overwhelmingly white and middle class, may have similar repercussions.

This phenomenon is even more marked on the state's community

college campuses, where the overwhelming number of minority students feels that the college and its resources are there to be used to achieve concrete personal objectives.

A note of cautious and realistic optimism is difficult to repress when one considers what is actually happening on community college campuses in respect to the poor. Pasadena City College, for example, has taken over a large industrial plant convenient to the minority community and refitted it as a Community Adult Training Center. The Center runs from 8 A.M. until 10 P.M. each weekday and half-days on Saturday. Over 4,000 people are taking classes in such fields as appliance service, supermarket merchandising, and aeronautics ground school. In the first 15 months of the Center's operation, 717 people were placed directly in permanent jobs during a period of economic recession for the state as a whole.

Another hopeful aspect to this picture is the total number of minority students who have elected to take advantage of community college education with or without any form of assistance. Of roughly 300,000 full-time students attending California Community Colleges, 67,000 were from minority groups and of these 42,000 are from families with incomes under $5,000 per year. Thus, these institutions on the whole have not only met, but exceeded, previous state guidelines for integration of public schools (15 percent). This has been accomplished with little fuss or public controversy. That is, minority students have been recruited and made to feel welcome without compromising the rights or legitimate interests of the Caucasian majority. The fact that almost 70,000 Black and Mexican-American students were attending California Community Colleges is one which has immense consequences for the near future. For most of these students will inevitably become members of a growing middle class among minority groups, a middle class that must emerge and lead if the threat of a polarized and racially divided America is to be overcome.

The reader is asked to summon his imaginative resources to appreciate what these necessarily cold and prosaic numbers mean in human terms. In virtually every community in the state there are now hundreds, often thousands, of young people from poverty-stricken homes and culturally deprived backgrounds who, instead of hanging around street corners waiting for the "connection" or cruising about the streets looking for "the action," are in school learning and planning, preparing themselves to enter fields like medicine and law and technology. While learning fundamental skills, they are also acquiring an appreciation of their own culture and history and learning to relate that culture and history to their proper place in the development of American society. Each day they return home, where they offer a tangible alternative to their younger brothers and sisters to the traditional lures of the street gangs and hustlers. If programs such as EOPS are continued and expanded for another decade, Californians will see an immense change for the better in the problems associated with the ghettos, poverty, welfare, crime, and narcotics addiction within that decade.

Of course, a good many problems remain. First, there is the lack of funds. But quite apart from monetary limitations, some inherent difficulties have already begun to emerge in the first trial years of EOPS. Perhaps the most serious of these is the attitude that caused the problem in the first place: our all too human tendency to build walls against and around what is different and "other." Even within a program fundamentally aimed at achieving integration, segregation takes place. A few administrators may have hired a Black or a Chicano to "run the program for the minority kids" and more or less washed their hands of the matter, except for budgetary considerations. A few faculty members may be content to "let the minorities do their thing," a "thing" presumed to be outside the regular college program. Some minority students tend to cling together. None of these things necessarily springs from some evil intent. In many cases it is a matter of the traditional notion of live and let live. But the cumulative effect could undermine a fundamental goal of the entire program—true integration and equality.

Also, some Caucasian students may have developed a somewhat defensive attitude toward the appearance on campus of large numbers of minority students. The philosophy underlying the EOPS program—that society should take an extra step in helping the poor escape from their poverty—may not be understood completely by the ordinary middle-class Caucasian, who wonders why minority students get grants or special tutoring when he may have to pay his own college expenses.

Finally the general public, which looks at the costs, both human and financial, of social programs is sometimes suspicious of direct attempts to ameliorate these problems by "do-gooders" and "bleeding hearts." There is a need for the people running various EOPS programs to be mindful of public sensibilities and to avoid even the appearance of waste and frivolity. The answer to any complaints of extravagance can be found in one simple fact—the average expenditure for each EOPS student in California is about $200 *per year*. Many of the services provided by EOPS, such as tutorial programs, are being purchased at bargain rates. Wages for tutors, for example, tend to be only slightly above the minimum wage level.

Reference has been made previously to the land-grant colleges and universities established in the nineteenth century with federal aid. At that time the government was concerned with the development of the frontier, the growth of agriculture, and tapping the rich resources of the still half-wild West. At least partially because of the leadership, research, and technology provided by what were in effect frontier colleges, American agriculture, mining, and allied arts quickly outperformed even the most extravagant hopes of those who were instrumental in creating these unique and, for the time, somewhat far-reaching institutions. American farms and orchards and mines became veritable cornucopias from which flowed an almost limitless abundance. The investment of the community colleges in the minds and spirits of those who happen to be young and poor may bear a similar harvest one day. In a very real sense there is a new gold rush in California today. And we mine not yellow metal, but the intellectual and spiritual resources of the people. We believe the state as a whole is going to strike it rich. Remember that it was the poor, the dispossessed, the disinherited, and the refugees who built the United States and this state. And when those who happen to be at the bottom rise, they lift the entire structure of society with them.

4

OCCUPATIONAL EDUCATION

For many decades vocational education called occupational education in many California Community Colleges), like economy in government, while widely praised and frequently hailed as the solution to many of our economic and social woes, has been more honored in the breach than the observance. Public opinion polls have shown repeatedly that the great majority of Americans have believed that colleges should concentrate more heavily on the practical, i.e., money-making, aspects of education. Industrial and political leaders, while sometimes critical of educational frills, have been traditionally willing to support job-training and job-creating programs. Most students have listed career training and preparation for a job as their primary objectives in seeking higher education.

Nevertheless, occupational education has not always sailed under brisk and favorable winds. A lingering prejudice associating occupational training with social inferiority has sometimes proven a handicap among parents, students, and faculty. Some institutions avoided a substantial commitment to the occupational aspects of their educational program lest they be regarded as "trade schools." Why the trade school image has been so poor is not easy to understand. Perhaps it has something to do with the fact that in the past high school students who were deemed unable or unwilling to master academic subjects were often transferred to "shop classes" if they were boys or to home economics courses if girls.

Also, it may have something to do with America's democratic social tradition. In more structured western countries, such as Germany, where only a small percentage of the total youth population, usually those deemed wellborn or academically gifted, were allowed to go to college, and where the bulk of the population was expected to concentrate on vocational education as a matter of course, the trade schools carry no such stigma. But perhaps because Americans take the concept of equal educational opportunity more seriously than most, they have traditionally shunned trade schools and courses deemed second best.

In a variety of ways, the California Community Colleges have worked hard to overcome this prejudice. Partly as the result of their own efforts, partly because of growing sophistication about education among students and the general public, and partly because of the encouragement of local boards of trustees and the Board of Governors of the California Community Colleges, occupational education has enjoyed remarkable growth in the very recent past. Traditionally, academic transfer students have made up the heavy majority of community college enrollments. In 1964, for example, occupational students accounted for 42 percent of total community college enrollment. Now they make up about 60 percent of the students. Since 1959 occupational education has leaped forward an astonishing 259 percent, and just since 1968 it has grown 25 percent. It is clearly the most rapidly expanding aspect of the two-year college program. California Community Colleges now offer over 3,200 programs, covering virtually every occupation—from semiskilled to highly skilled technicians to paraprofessional—that makes a major impact on the state's economy and on the lives of its 20,000,000 citizens. This education is in-service and preservice as well as retraining.

To bring about this change, these institutions have wisely insisted on fully equal status for both students and faculty in occupational education programs. They have also provided opportunities in "career education" for people who do not wish to be frozen into one job or even one profession for a lifetime. Great emphasis is placed on mobility. For example, a young man with a fondness for the outdoors may wish to become a forester. But perhaps he lacks the resources, at this time, to pursue a full four-year forestry course. Also the fact is that at present the demand for graduate foresters is relatively light, while there is a much greater need for what the federal government calls "forest technicians." These are people with an associate of arts or science degree or its equivalent who can supervise forest workers under the direction of a professional forester. The young man may decide to take courses at any number of community colleges that will qualify him to work as a forest technician. There is, of course, nothing to prevent him from going on, either by going to evening classes or by enrolling full time at a four-year college at a later date. And when he does complete his forestry training, he will have an enormous advantage in the competition for available openings because he already has had practical experience. Finally, his educational experience will probably be enriched by his ability to relate what is being said in the classroom to what is being done in the field.

"Lifelong learning" has been an established slogan in American education for many decades. Millions of our citizens have learned to speak and write the English language and master the fundamentals of our national heritage in evening classes. Tens of millions have acquired useful skills in such classes, from drafting to law to sophisticated electronics engineering. The community colleges have a great commitment to offer continuing education courses in convenient locations. They offer scores of certificate programs of less than two years

for those who want to learn a specific skill and go to work as soon as possible. Many of these students return for additional education. What is unique about the community college's effort in occupational education is the structuring, not merely of courses, but also of programs and the integration of these programs with the ebb and flow of economic needs and forces. Thus, each of these institutions has many business and industry advisory committees that feed current and practical information to the college as to what skills are needed by local firms, offer follow-up information on the success of graduates of existing programs, and provide a strong basis for support of the college program in the various complex problems that inevitably arise. The strength of occupational programs rests on the advice and support of these local groups.

California's two-year colleges have pushed hard for occupational education, partly because it fulfills a real need for both students and the community, but also because it is good for the college. Such programs generate support for the total college program by influential government, business, and labor leaders, and the media—all of whom can perhaps more readily perceive the utility of occupational programs than, say, courses in the philosophy of the French Enlightenment. And one consequence is that these institutions are thus enabled to offer more and better courses that are purely academic in nature.

The integrated approach to occupational education may well represent a more fundamental and profound development in higher education than even its most ardent champions realize. It may well portend sweeping changes in all levels of American education, particularly in the high schools and in the four-year colleges. To understand why this may be so, it is necessary to review briefly some of the specific problems of the American economy at the present time, or at least those problems relating directly to higher education.

For many decades the United States enjoyed a favorable balance of trade in the world, meaning simply that we sold more goods abroad than we bought, despite the fact that Americans have traditionally been the world's highest paid workers. We were able to overcome the disadvantage of high labor costs because of enormous advantages in productive skill and because we were the world's leader in both capital and in the technology to put that capital to work on a basis that could compete favorably with other industrial nations. After World War II the United States began to export both capital and technology. That is, we sent workers all over the world to teach our methods of production, and we sent businessmen all over the world to invest in foreign enterprises. Also, thousands of bright young people came from various friendly nations to study at our schools and colleges. As a result, nations that had been our customers gradually became our competitors in the world market. The favorable balance of trade shifted to an unfavorable balance, and jobs were lost by Americans for this and other reasons. At the same time the process known as automation was making it possible for fewer people to produce far more goods.

The United States has suffered a somewhat severe rate of unemployment more or less continuously for many years. The problem has been most acute among young people, who have experienced two or three times as high a rate of unemployment as the rest of the population. Moreover, the problem has approached the crisis level among minority-group youth. In many of the nation's ghettos unemployment levels of 30 percent or higher are a fact of life.

While this unemployment persists and while foreign economic competition grows more formidable each year, a glance at the classified ads of any metropolitan newspaper will quickly confirm that there is no shortage of jobs in many parts of the American economy. There is instead a gulf between the needs of employers for highly skilled and trained people and the large numbers of unemployed and perhaps unemployable people—particularly young people.

This gulf has created a serious imbalance in the economy and much human suffering and waste of human resources. Young people, particularly those in the various ethnic and racial minorities, arrive at that point in life where energy, idealism, and hope are running strongest—when, in a sense, they have more to give society than they will ever have again, and when their need to feel part of the community and to affirm self-worth through constructive labor is greatest —only to be faced with "no help wanted" signs. The result has been millions of potentially useful young men and women being forced to spend their best years standing on street corners—quick and easy prey for the pusher, the hustler, and the agitator. Apart from the human tragedy implicit in these facts, the social and economic and political costs of this army of unwanted youth, if the total could be computed accurately, would probably be as great or greater than any other national problem—including defense.

The existence of these unemployed young people partly underlies the "law and order" issue, nourishes the drug business, and exacerbates racial tensions to the point where both sides become polarized. It may not be mere coincidence that one American president and two candidates for president were shot by young men with a somewhat similar pattern of drifting about the fringes of the economy without being able to find something useful and meaningful to do. Had someone found a way to bring the Sirhans, Oswalds, and Bremers into the economy, their victims might never have been attacked. What is true in these highly visible and publicized cases is no less true of tens of thousands of incidents in which the victims are not well known.

One specific and positive step being taken toward amelioration of this problem can be cited. At some community colleges regular members of the faculty are holding credit college-level courses in a variety of subjects *inside* correctional institutions. Thus it is possible for a young person, while serving time in prison, to accumulate a substantial number of credits toward a fully accredited degree. Prisoners, faculty members who teach the courses, and prison authorities have been highly pleased with the success of the program thus far.

Whether the program will result in a significant long-term drop in the rate of recidivism on the part of these inmates taking college courses, as measured against the rate for those who do not, must await further research. But clearly if only a handful of these young people can be redirected toward making a contribution to society rather than preying upon it, the relatively minor expense—not much more than the faculty member's salary—to the taxpayer will have reaped enormous benefit.

No society is so rich or so automated that it can afford not to use the energy and talents of its young people. Sociologists have affirmed that at least one of the causative factors behind the "hippie" phenomenon has been a feeling on the part of a great many young people that they are simply human surplus whose contribution to the economy and to society is not particularly wanted or needed.

As the cliché has it, the road to hell is often paved with good intentions. Those who fought hard for laws outlawing child labor and for higher minimum wages usually acted with the best of motives: they wished to protect people who could not protect themselves against exploitation. But as so often happens, there were unforeseen consequences of these essentially benevolent and necessary acts. For many centuries in western Europe and America, a system had evolved that prepared the young generation to take over the work of their elders. This was the apprenticeship system. A young man, upon completing his formal education at whatever age, would be apprenticed to an older worker or group of workers and gradually learn the trade or business or profession in which he was destined to spend his working life. The youth had the advantage of a practical education and a sense of increasing usefulness. The worker or businessman had the advantage of human energy and intelligence at negligible cost. With the organization of labor and industry, plus the impact of federal legislation that indirectly made it uneconomic to hire the young and inexperienced and the introduction of machinery to do much of the "fetch and carry" kind of work that apprentices used to do, the apprenticeship system is not as strong in the United States as in other countries. The schools have tried to take up the slack. But they quickly discovered that not all young people readily adapted to and benefited from formal classroom instruction or even from occupational education conducted in an artificial environment. At a certain point in life a young man needs the experience of "playing for keeps"—of knowing that what he does will be measured in the cold and objective judgment not of sympathetic parents or even teachers, but of the marketplace.

Community colleges have become increasingly aware of this need. Many have responded by instituting a new kind of on-the-job training that manages to overcome many of the purely economic barriers to such programs by a combination of local, state, and federal resources used in cooperation with local business. Good examples of this program are those in a number of community colleges in which the student works 30 hours a week and carries a 12-unit college load. He may receive four units for his supervised work program, which is divided into one unit for lectures and three units for work experience. The lectures are organized around his work experience and problems. In addition he takes two courses designed to develop job skills.

Such programs have now expanded to most community colleges and are growing very rapidly with the assistance of state funding which recently was made available for work-experience education. Federal funding has added millions of dollars to California's secondary and community college vocational education programs. Federal funding for vocational education in community colleges increased from about $10 million in 1970–71 to about $12 million in 1972–73. New federal funding would make feasible even greater expansion. In addition, the Board of Governors is presently reviewing ways of providing even greater financial incentives to promote and encourage such programs in the community colleges.

There is every reason to believe that the impact of such programs on the nation's domestic economy and on the ability of Americans to compete in foreign markets will be substantial, if not critical. Over a century ago the leaders of Prussia decided to make Germany the strongest power in Europe. They decided to accomplish this aim by investing heavily in an educational program that would make the German worker the most productive and skilled in Europe. However much we may deplore the ultimate ends to which the Prussians put this program, the fact that it worked can hardly be disputed. Germany's miraculous recovery from her virtual destruction and dismemberment in World War II can be attributed in large part to the fact that a nation whose people have mastered the skills necessary to compete successfully in the modern world will almost inevitably become prosperous in an era of peace.

The simple fact is that the American worker, given his high standard of living, must outproduce his counterpart in Europe or Asia and—in the not too distant future, Africa—if our economy is to continue to prosper. And since human labor is finite, while human knowledge is infinite, the best hope for continued prosperity is through more and better education and training in the specific skills needed to make a technological society function.

This sounds a great deal easier than in fact it is. The purely educational and technical barriers to the effective implementation of such programs are, relatively, the easiest to overcome. Even the financial limitations are gradually receding as society comes to understand more about the need for united action rather than simply "lifting oneself up by one's own bootstraps." For it is becoming clear that this was a great deal easier to do when America was a nation with a chronic shortage of labor rather than a surplus of it. "Bootstrapping"

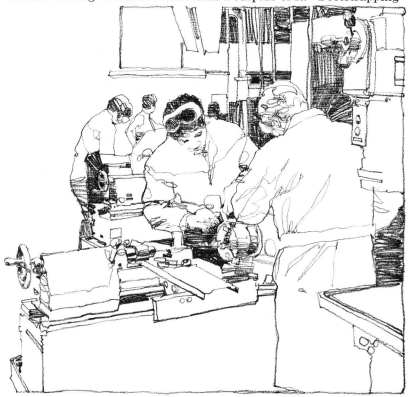

was easier when the young "greenhorn" fresh off the boat from Europe could go to almost any factory and, merely by using the strength of his back and the muscles in his arms, earn an honest living, however meager. Today "muscle power" alone is not in very high demand.

Perhaps the most serious kinds of problems faced by California's Community Colleges in attempting to expand their occupational education programs probably stem from a purely human factor—the resistance of men and institutions to change. Some employers may continue to harbor ancient prejudices about what is and is not "white man's work." Although these men are a small and dwindling minority, ancient prejudices die hard, and their effect lingers. For Mexican-Americans to work in the field is considered normal by some, but for them to operate sophisticated farm machinery sometimes meets silent but dogged resistance. Also important is the attitude of labor unions, many of which have shown a similar pattern of resistance to change, in effect if not in rhetoric. Young people of minority backgrounds know that barriers have existed and are therefore reluctant to undertake long and arduous training programs to prepare themselves to enter a field where access may be blocked, not by lack of ability but by skin color or accent. The Community Colleges Board of Governors, mindful of such problems, has taken the position that it will not be a party to policies that are exclusionary rather than democratic. Some trades, where the needs and rewards could be greatest for both society and the invidivual worker, are sealed off by the exercise of power for ends that are inconsistent with a democratic society. Thus educators embarking on occupational training programs have to walk a thin line between the needs and interests of employers, labor unions, and the students themselves.

Finally, there is the overriding interest of society at large to be considered. For example, everyone who drives an automobile in California, which is practically every adult in the state, is sooner or later made aware of his dependence on the skill, honesty, and reliability of the automobile mechanic. Many of America's great automotive geniuses began by tinkering with the family car and hanging around garages until they learned almost everything there was to know about the mysteries of the automobile. But it is also true that a good many incompetents were "educated" in exactly the same way. The trouble has been that it is impossible for most ordinary drivers to know whether the young man who works on their car is a budding Henry Ford or someone about to turn a minor problem into a major disaster.

Proper occupational education cannot eliminate such problems, but it can reduce them and give the public a measure of security. It can also advance the state of art.

The great prosperity of California has derived in no small measure from the willingness of its people to enter into a strange, new technological wilderness and exploit what they find in a practical way. The great wealth generated for the people of the state by the motion picture, aerospace, and electronics industries, and the pioneering work done here in scientific farming are all examples of the growth of multibillion dollar empires in fields that were all but nonexistent a few years earlier. The future well-being of the state depends upon the ability to continue to foster attitudes of mind and habits of workmanship that will create tomorrow's economic miracles, just as the movies and electronics transformed so many lives in the recent past. In this effort the community colleges will inevitably play a critical role. As the only segment of public higher education in the state legally empowered to offer one- and two-year programs that are explicitly vocational, these two-year colleges must supply the technicians and middle-management people to staff businesses and industries and farms. They must also train growing numbers of those who work at the subprofessional level in rapidly expanding fields of human services such as paramedicine. Since the supply of physicians in the United States cannot in the near future meet the rising demand for health services, only by training large numbers of subprofessional medical people to deliver health services under the physician's direction can we begin to solve what has been called the nation's number one problem—the problem of staying alive and healthy.

Traditionally, most Americans have placed the work ethic at or near the top of their list of fundamental social values. Most would agree with Thomas Carlyle that "There is a perennial nobleness, and even sacredness in Work.... Blessed is he who has found his work." Perhaps the aversion to the economic burden of welfare does not account for the widespread distaste of the welfare program as much as does the feeling of many Americans that not to work is to be deprived of one of the most profound sources of human happiness and satisfaction.

The community colleges, primarily middle-class institutions reflecting dominant middle-class values, tend to agree. They stress occupation precisely because they do indeed see some "perennial nobleness" in helping people to find a satisfying and rewarding vocation. A few years ago it was popular in some circles to urge young people to drop out of the world of work and spend their time contemplating Higher Things. It was no surprise that many of those unfortunate youngsters who took this shallow advice wound up trying to fill the empty hours with drugs, crime, and various affronts to human dignity—all in the name of a Higher Consciousness.

Few community college students or faculty members have ever taken such ideas seriously. They understand that work is not only a means of earning a livelihood, but, particularly in an industrial civilization, a fundamental means of relating to both the social and the natural world, and of expressing that creative instinct, that desire to do something of value, which is present in one form or another in all human beings.

5

CAMPUS AND COMMUNITY

If one reviews the great political struggles that both divided and united the United States prior to 1960, the astonishing thing is how small a role most of the nation's educational institutions played in these battles. The struggle for independence from Britain, the rise of Jacksonian prairie democracy, the Civil War, the development of America's great corporate empires and the consequent organization of the nation's working people into national unions, the New Deal, America's participation in World War II and subsequent leadership of the noncommunist world—few if any of these movements were particularly academic in origin, style, or leadership. Individual professors and former professors, and a few students, did of course, play leadership roles here and there. But no one familiar with the history, organization, and dominant characteristics of higher education in America was likely to have predicted the explosion of political interest and activity that characterized the campus in the late sixties and early seventies.

In retrospect it is easy to see many reasons why the campuses were so quiet during most of this nation's first two centuries of national existence. For one thing, Americans have always tended to idealize youth and hence prolong it as much as possible. In Europe people in their late teens and early twenties have traditionally been considered to be young men and women. Americans thought of the same group as "teenagers." (The word itself is of American origin.) When the authors were in college, campus heroes and heroines were athletes and beauty queens—rarely scholars or political activists. Campus humor centered on "petting" and writing home for money. Professors with strongly held political ideas were not plentiful. In short, the overwhelming majority of students and faculty accepted the notion of the campus as an "ivory tower"—remote, lovely, detached from bitter partisan struggles waged elsewhere.

And if prior to the 1960s the campus was largely nonpolitical, it was also true that politics in this century was largely nonintellectual. American politicians were more preoccupied with the pragmatic problems of the Depression, winning the war against Hitler and Tojo, and achieving peace between management and labor than with ideological issues.

This pattern began to change when, in the wake of post-World War II affluence, millions of hitherto excluded young people from once poor families began to go to college. The massive increase in quantity brought about subtle changes in the quality and nature of academic life. A revolution in the media, particularly the rise of television, brought about a sharply increased level of political awareness and sophistication on the part of the young. Politics became popular, and political leaders like young President Kennedy were surrounded by an aura of "star quality." "Charisma" became the name of the game. Finally, the issues themselves shifted from largely economic concerns to those of civil rights, America's proper role in world affairs, the growth of a governmental bureaucracy—ideas rather than things—and hence more interesting to people whose primary business was to teach and learn ideas.

The public first became aware of the change when many students emerged as leaders in the early freedom rides in the deep South. Most of them deliberately broke Southern laws and violated Southern customs, seeking a confrontation with authority. Many went to jail. A new kind of hero began to emerge on a handful of the nation's urban university campuses: the freedom rider.

In 1964 in San Francisco the Republicans nominated conservative Barry Goldwater to run for the presidency. The campus of the University of California at nearby Berkeley became a focal point for anti-Goldwater agitation and activities. After a time, university authorities, under a barrage of complaints from Bay Area business people and others who had been the target of student political activism, sought to restrain political activity on the campus. They acted under the assumption that a public university campus was not an appropriate place for partisan politics. The result was the Free Speech Movement of 1964. The rest of the story is familiar. Disturbances spread from campus to campus, group to group, cause to cause. By the late sixties students and professors were embroiled in politics as never before. The role of the American campus in active politics had changed course almost 180 degrees.

At present every element of higher education in America, and particularly in California, is struggling to learn to live with this altered reality—and with its consequences. Californians, acting through their elected officials, have a history of dealing generously with higher education. As a result, the University of California, the California State University and Colleges, and the California Community Colleges became the unquestioned pacesetters for the nation in public, tax-supported higher education. Few questioned that California was—quite simply—the best. Other states set out to reorganize their own higher educational systems on the California model. In some states public colleges and universities were dominated by politicians who used the prestige, resources, and budgets of the colleges to reward their friends and enhance their own political futures. During the decade of the thirties Californians were both amused and—if they thought about it—a little shocked to see pictures of Louisiana governor "Kingfish" Huey Long sitting on the bench during football games calling LSU's plays. The Kingfish did publicly what others did privately. But in California locally elected nonpartisan and nonpolitical boards of trustees called the plays insofar as governance of the community colleges was concerned. The guardians of the state's higher educational institutions assiduously avoided, for the most part, participating in partisan politics. The public responded with wholehearted and generous support.

Much of this tradition was swept away in the angry wake of the New Politics, which often as not centered in and around a college campus. Polls indicated that at least 90 percent of the general public vigorously disapproved of the riots and tumult that erupted on campus. Financial support from political leaders began to slip away. Tax overrides were turned down by the voters. Professional educators, with no particular partisan axe to grind, were caught between campus militants demanding often extreme and shocking actions, and a public that believed firmly that schools existed to prepare young people for careers, not to change the nation's social institutions. The watchword for educators during much of this period was sheer survival.

In a certain sense the California Community Colleges were relatively fortunate during these years of storm and stress. By their very nature they were and are uniquely designed to meet many of the problems that lie at the root of our troubles in higher education. For one thing, these institutions have no elitist tradition. As Professors Medsker and Tillery have noted in a report prepared for the Carnegie Commission on Higher Education, the community colleges have always regarded themselves as "People's Colleges." Free and open access, one of the burning issues on the four-year campuses in recent years, is guaranteed as a matter of law in each of the state's 96 community colleges. "Local control," a slogan of some campus militants, is also a traditional fact of life at the two-year colleges. The cry for "relevance" in higher education, which resounded throughout the nation in the late 1960s, surprised a good many community college instructors and students because relevance to the needs and interests of the student has long been characteristic of these campuses. In short, the typical community college already embodies in its usual practices many of the "reforms" sought at other institutions throughout the nation and around the world. These practices were adopted, not as a matter of reform, but as a matter of common sense by the people who organized local colleges to meet the immediate objectives of local citizens.

For these reasons, plus others that may have played a role, the community colleges have emerged from the past few years of turmoil and violence somewhat shaken and changed, but relatively unscathed. They have rarely, if ever, operated on anything resembling a factory system. Generally, their administrators, instructors, and students, like those at other institutions of higher education in the state, know each other, meet and speak to one another as human beings, and therefore are not likely to start throwing bricks at one another. While there are some exceptions, it is fair to assert that in the main faculty-student relations at most community colleges are characterized by mutual respect and good will.

Perhaps the most complicated—and certainly the most sensitive—area of statewide community college work is dealing with the number of independent and diverse agencies, branches of government, educational segments, and interest groups, each with its own set of purposes and rightful interests. Advancing the cause of the community colleges requires systematic and planned contacts with all levels of state and federal government, statewide educational segments, business and industry and labor, as well as community college trustees, faculty, students, and administrators. Balancing these competitive interests while maintaining overall good will and enhancing the general perception of the community colleges are continuing concerns of the Board of Governors when engaged in statewide decision making.

By and large, the community colleges start out with a plus in terms of perception: these two-year institutions are responsive to their local communities—and therefore obviously "accountable"—costs are low, quality and productivity are high, and technical as well as academic programs are available on all campuses. As a result, California legislators are generally happy with these colleges for many reasons, one of which is that their constituents are usually pleased with their local campuses.

Community colleges have worked hard at low cost, high quality education and avoided academic status-seeking. As a result, they are perceived by the public as institutions that are not ambitious to become four-year colleges, that are close to the people, and that as a rule are just as concerned with spending a dollar as the taxpayer is.

Building on that base of high productivity, insistence on teaching, and emphasis on employment as a student goal, the two-year colleges have generally found that state government has been sympathetic to and understanding of their unique characteristics. Although no one associated with the California Community Colleges can say that these institutions have been financed adequately, there is some comfort in knowing that lack of adequate financing is not a result of hostility. Unsuccessful local tax elections, for example, arise more often from the frustration of property-tax payers than from animosity toward the local campus.

Community college needs, of course, are not considered by state government out of context with those of other segments of education: elementary and secondary education, California State University and Colleges, the University of California, and the independent colleges and universities. All of these interests, plus the general public, are represented on the Coordinating Council for Higher Education, a state agency designed to provide advice to state government and higher education. The Council has provided a forum for community colleges to air issues related to other segments of education in the state. By and large, the members of the Coordinating Council have shown a strong disposition toward the community college concepts of comprehensive campuses and local management of these campuses.

In addition, the community colleges deal directly with the other segments of education. In vocational education—a concern and responsibility of high schools as well as two-year colleges—both these segments work closely together to determine how federal funds are divided in the state and how the programs are managed. Three members each from the State Board of Education and the Board of Governors of the California Community Colleges, plus the State Superintendent of Public Instruction and the Chancellor of the California Community Colleges, are members of the state's Joint Committee on Vocational Education. This committee meets regularly to resolve issues in this field involving these two segments of education in the state.

In transfer programs, which affect the ability of two-year college students to transfer to four-year campuses in the state, community colleges have worked hard to make sure that transfer students are treated equitably with "native students" in the four-year colleges and that all appropriate academic credit is transferred without loss. One result of this effort is a recent adoption by the Regents of the University of California that the University accept transfer students from community colleges with 56 units of work and a 2.0 ("C") average. In the past the University had required a 2.4 grade average. Another result is a recent agreement with the California State University and Colleges for better accommodations for community college transfer students.

Since a major function of the community colleges is to train students for direct employment, a great deal of effort goes into good working relationships with business and industry and labor. All technical and occupational programs at the campus level are developed and conducted in consultation with practitioners and managers in each employment field. Campus representatives work closely with local business and labor leaders, as do community college representatives at the state level. Because of those efforts and the demand for community college-trained personnel, the California Community Colleges and business and industry leaders have been able to count on each other for support at critical times.

Nor can the many and different needs and demands of the various elements within the community colleges be ignored or given secondary treatment. Perhaps because of the statewide decentralization of the community colleges, they represent a very diverse segment of education. For in addition to the interests of faculty, students, and administrators, there are also the direct considerations of over 400 individual trustees and 69 different boards of trustees—as well as the interests of a multiplicity of communities and local and regional groups.

The trustees are simply citizens whose only vested interests are those of their local communities and community colleges. Although it might appear that dealing with still another large group of individuals would be merely an additional responsibility for the Board of Governors, actually the very existence of the trustees, individually and as district boards, makes the job of coalescing and communicating with all local interests much easier. The reason is that the trustees themselves represent diverse community groups: local chambers of commerce, taxpayers associations, homeowners groups, fraternal organizations, and others. Trustees are elected to office for four-year terms and, as such, have every reason to speak for the many and varied interest groups in their communities.

In large communities it is not uncommon to have as many as 20 or 30 candidates running for trustee offices, and one district has had well over 100 candidates in a single election. This too represents a profound change from the time when a college trustee's job was considered largely ceremonial and honorific.

Today's local trustee often finds himself making critical decisions, often before angry and sometimes hostile groups of competing local citizens. His job is all the more demanding because these citizens are his neighbors. There is a bromide in the newspaper business to the effect that it is easy to write an editorial criticizing a politician thousands of miles away who will in all likelihood not bother to read the editorial; but it is another matter to criticize a local businessman or official whom one is likely to run into at lunch that very afternoon.

Because the members of the Board of Governors of the California Community Colleges believe strongly in local control and because of the desire of trustees to have a significant statewide impact on what happens to the community colleges, local trustees have become increasingly active in recent years, both in terms of individual activity and of organizational participation. Advice from the trustees is sought because they generally have no axe to grind except that of the ordinary citizen and taxpayer of the state. The Board of Governors relates easily to local trustees because they are all lay citizens, not professional educators, and as such understand each other well and share similar concerns and interests.

In recent years community college faculty have also organized more actively in various groups. Instructors have demonstrated their concern with and ability to promote improvements overall, not just within the narrow interests of any one college or academic group. Faculty are widely consulted on all levels of affairs, locally on academic and evaluation matters, and statewide on significant matters involving all community college interests.

Students in the California Community Colleges have surprised many observers by their active participation in statewide and legislative matters—"surprised" because in the past students in two-year institutions did not become active organizationally until they had transferred to four-year campuses. Not so in California, where students are interested in and vocal on most matters concerning community college affairs.

Notwithstanding the activity and interests of all other community college segments, administrators, particularly district superintendents and college presidents, need to be consulted regularly and frequently, for it is they who are directly responsible on a day-to-day basis for the management of these campuses. By and large, the main concern of administrators, of course, is for their own campuses, but they are also concerned with and involved in decisions affecting all the community colleges in the state.

Consultation with these diverse and sometimes competing elements takes different forms. With representatives of the state executive and legislative branches, effective consultation tends to be irregular and informal, with the frequency dependent upon the situation. Consultation with representatives of community colleges and affiliated organizations, on the other hand, is more regular, with trustees, faculty, students, and administrators often meeting together as advisory committees to discuss future planning, as well as current and pressing issues.

There are many community college organizations in the state representing virtually every interest. The California Junior College Association is made up of trustees, students, faculty, and administrators. Trustees are represented by the Community College Section of the California School Boards Association and by the Association of Community College Trustees. Students are represented by the California Community College Student Government Association. Faculty are represented by the California Teachers Association, the Faculty Association of the California Community Colleges, the Academic Senate of the California Community Colleges, the California Federation of Teachers, and the American Association of University Professors. In addition, there are significant and active associations representing administrators, classified (noncredentialed) employees, business and facilities officials, deans of instruction and vocational education, deans of continuing education and student services, counselors, librarians, public relations officers, directors of extended opportunities and services, financial-aid and job-placement officers, and those involved in athletics and individual instructional disciplines. Although it is not possible to carry out all the divergent recommendations made by each and every one of these groups, the opportunity to listen to such advice is an absolute necessity because of the expertise and knowledge of attitudes and experience that come into play as a result.

All of these groups are concerned with and involved in the California legislature's present study of the state's Magna Carta of higher education—the Master Plan of Higher Education adopted in 1960. In a difficult time of very rapid growth, political upheaval, and acute budgetary crisis, the Master Plan has served the state, the people, and the colleges well. However, the time has clearly come for updating. Suggestions had been made earlier for the consolidation of all three segments of California's existing tripartite system of higher education (University of California, California State University and

Colleges, and California Community Colleges) into a single system under a unified "superboard." Proposals of this kind sometimes have a certain appeal, since they seem to promise more orderly and efficient administration and less wrangling in the ranks. However, as many people have learned in working with other superboards in government, and in business or labor for that matter, the results may often be the direct opposite of the original purpose of consolidating and concentrating power. Governance becomes more remote and cumbersome, and less responsive to demands for change. Existing conflicts of men and issues do not simply disappear; the struggles continue in the corridors of bureaucratic power.

The present system of local, community control of the community colleges is the very heart of their success. It would be a mistake for the state to abolish or seriously restrict this system by transferring decision-making power from local to state authorities.

A major problem that plagued higher education from the very inception of the Master Plan was the problem of articulation, that is, of transferability of credit from one institution to another. A superboard that would deal with the problem by executive decree is one answer to the problem, but it is not the correct or most viable answer. As the result of direct negotiations between the concerned parties, substantial progress in solving this problem has been made in recent years. The aforementioned actions of the University of California and the California State University and Colleges in respect to community college transfer students are concrete signs of progress. The continuing success of community college transfer students has worn away the resistance of all but the diehard few who take the position that "if we didn't teach it, obviously it hasn't been taught properly."

There has also been a growing demand on the part of the public for "accountability." That is, faculty and students must demonstrate that taxpayer funds are being used for socially worthwhile purposes, not wasted in indulging frills and unnecessary pet projects. "Accountability" must begin with the people directly involved, faculty and students. There are problems in this involvement unique to the community colleges. Students with only two years' residence on a given campus often lack strong identification with that institution and may lack the experience to play as strong a role as might be desired.

Finally, there may be those who seek to "politicize" the campus in one cause or another by "capturing it" for a particular cause, candidate, or philosophy. While these people obviously have every right to be partisan in their private lives, they sometimes fail to grasp that the state's colleges are supported and maintained by Democrats and Republicans, by liberals and moderates and conservatives, and by persons of almost every conceivable race, religion, and philosophy. Under our system no one should have the right to make a tax-supported college a monolith, in the image of a single creed or cause. If the colleges reflect only the liberal point of view, for example, then others will sooner or later attack them. And vice versa. It is simply asking too much to expect people to pay dearly to support views they hold to be the doctrine of the devil unless their own views are assured of a fair hearing as well. It would be folly to expect college instructors to teach only what is popular with the majority. It would also be folly for instructors to teach only what is offensive to the majority. The business of education is to find and teach truth, not one view of the truth.

This problem was more or less peripheral when colleges were few and students a small minority of their age group. With the proliferation of campuses and the advent of mass enrollments, it has become central to the whole educative process. As Marshall McLuhan has pointed out, moving information in one form or another is likely to become the most important and largest business in America in the not too distant future, if indeed it has not become that already. Surely the colleges are up to their necks in the information business. Hence they have themselves moved from the periphery to the center of the political, economic, and social stage.

The dominant fact in American domestic life in the period between the Civil War and the Great Depression was the rise of corporate business and the demand by the public for the products of business. In the 1930s and 1940s the labor unions led a movement toward concerns with personal and social welfare and security. In the late 1960s and in the 1970s the demand for more and more education may play a similar role as the center of action in American life. The profound dislocations of the past few years have reflected the attempt by society and by professional educators to adapt to the altered facts of life. The remote and lovely "ivory tower" campus is gone, possibly forever. What the cathedral was to the Middle Ages, what the palace was to the Renaissance, what the factory was to the nineteenth century, the campus is to our age. Thus it is not surprising that many of the fiercest political battles of our time seem to revolve around higher education.

Within this larger social ferment, community colleges have a unique and significant role to play. For the time is already at hand when the majority of our citizens will spend at least some time attending community college classes, including continuing education, and their cultural and social events. Community colleges exist to afford every citizen an opportunity not only to learn but also to participate in and contribute to the life of his village, town, or city.

6

FACULTY
AND STUDENTS

U nder the Master Plan for Higher Education, the California Community Colleges were granted full and equal partnership in California's tripartite system of higher education. Despite the principles of the Master Plan, community college students sometimes were the subject of something less than fully equal treatment when they sought to transfer to upper-division work. Despite a statement of the Coordinating Council for Higher Education that there be "no capricious or arbitrary barriers" to the transfer of community college students to four-year institutions, in fact such barriers existed until quite recently. Two factors have played a role in eliminating many, if not all, of these barriers. The first and most important undoubtedly has been the conspicuous success of community college transfer students. These students have been the subject of many studies.

One such study was instituted by George J. Maslach, former Dean of the College of Engineering and now Vice Chancellor at the University of California, Berkeley. His findings are as follows:

In the five years from 1963 through 1967, almost 35% of the students entering Berkeley's College of Engineering as juniors came from various community colleges in California; at times, transfer students have made up more than half the upper-division enrollment. These students have enjoyed such success in their studies at Berkeley that we welcome community college transfers wholeheartedly; their grade point average for all the courses they have taken at Berkeley is an outstanding 2.77, while in technical courses their performance gained them an average of 2.81. Moreover, one out of ten received honors at graduation, and 3% were awarded highest honors.

This record of achievement clearly shows the excellence of the preparation available at community colleges, and strongly supports the educational concept of the community college as an alternate path to the Bachelor of Science degree.

Even as the community college students are demonstrating their own and their instructors' abilities, the Board of Governors of the California Community Colleges has been firmly pressing for the removal of "artificial and capricious barriers" to the smooth transfer of these students to four-year institutions. The board's position has been that, if the partnership concept is to have real meaning, the four-year institutions should accept any course certified by a community college as transferable. That is, the community colleges should decide the academic merit of the courses they themselves offer. The board has preferred to seek voluntary agreement rather than state legislation to accomplish this end. The record of the students themselves and the logic of the argument, it was felt, would sooner or later carry the day.

It should also be noted that there is another important right granted community college students that, to our knowledge, is not shared by students at any accredited four-year college anywhere in the nation: the right to participate in the election of their own governing boards. With the passage of the law enabling 18-year-olds to vote, this right becomes very meaningful indeed. Anyone familiar with the typical pattern of board elections in most California Community Colleges will readily understand how easy it would be for the students at any given campus to unite behind a candidate or slate of candidates and carry the election.

Perhaps it should be quickly added that the chances of local boards being taken over by young extremists is rather remote because on virtually all two-year college campuses the students themselves reflect the values, economic groupings, interests, and ages of the total community. About half the students at any given community college are from 30 to 80 years of age, most of them taking one or two specific cources for specialized objectives. And even the remaining half of younger students tend to reflect dominant middle-class values, since most of them come from middle- and lower-middle-class homes.

Thus while "student power" is a legal fact and not a utopian educational objective at these institutions, that power has usually been used with restraint and intelligence, and there is little reason why this should not continue to be the case in the future. Community college administrators know now that their most important single constituency, politically speaking, is the people who take classes at the college. Nor, by and large, have faculty members used their considerable influence in an unprofessional manner to gain inappropriate advantages.

While there is no such thing as an average or typical community college student or instructor, the following is an attempt to draw a few composite and, hopefully, representative figures.

Student "A" is in his mid-twenties, married, a veteran, with one child. He has a part-time job; his wife also works. Neither is very well paid and, hence, even with his veteran's benefits their total income is probably below the national family average. They live in an apartment, drive an inexpensive car, and own a television set, which, however, they do not watch very often. Between jobs, family life, and school demands, they are very busy. Politically, student "A" is less liberal than his counterpart at, say, U.C. Berkeley, but more liberal than his parents. His IQ is above average, but his sociocultural background is something of a handicap, since he is the first member of his family to attend college. He does well in college, but only because he works hard at it. The college experience was rather bewildering to him at first and he thought seriously of quitting, but by the time he was well into his second year he had begun to acquire a genuine excitement about the subjects he was studying, particularly his major. He sees education primarily as the means to escape a routine, humdrum life and do some kind of work that will be more challenging, meaningful, and rewarding than that of his parents. His educational prognosis is excellent.

Student "B" is a young girl, a Mexican-American, who wishes to become a registered nurse. Her parents migrated from Mexico after World War II and her father works steadily, but his earnings are barely adequate to meet the needs of a large family. She, too, is the first member of her family to attend college, although several younger brothers and sisters are likely to follow if she is successful. She did well in high school, graduating with honors, and her decision to go to college stemmed from previous academic successes. Her parents resisted the decision at first, particularly her father, who felt apprehensive about his daughter pursuing a career rather than early marriage. The family is unable to help her with college expenses; she works part-time and receives minimal assistance from the college. She is a very good student, but has some problems that tend to originate in her cultural differences with the white, middle-class majority. Accepting dates from "Anglo" boys is one. She also has some difficulty about her relationships with some of the more militant campus Chicanos. She sympathizes with their objectives and is proud of many of their accomplishments, but finds their rhetoric and sometimes their tactics a bit hard to accept. Nevertheless, she spends part of her time tutoring younger Mexican-American students. Her chances of becoming a successful R.N. are outstanding.

Student "C" is a middle-class, white housewife in her forties. Her oldest children are in college, although she still has a younger one in high school. Her husband is a salesman, and they are buying a comfortable tract house. She started taking classes at her community college several years ago because a neighbor working toward a teaching credential urged her to, because she was bored watching television in the evening, and because she wanted to be able to share some of her children's college experiences. After several false starts, she found college work interesting and challenging. It provided a focal point for her middle years. Gradually she began to think about and finally accepted the idea of becoming a teacher. At this point she began attending day classes as well. Her official objective is still teaching, but she has begun secretly to wonder about going into graduate work to become a lawyer or taking a Ph.D. and trying to teach on the college level. She remembers how bored she was with

education two decades ago, how casually she dismissed the idea of going to college, and now wonders how she could have been so foolish. She devotes an enormous amount of time to her studies, which sometimes creates friction with her husband. The college experience has produced a good many changes in this woman. Her interests have expanded tremendously. Some of her old values have shifted so that behavior and ideas she might once have found shocking she now finds interesting or amusing. She has acquired some new friends among other women taking courses, and some of her older friends no longer seem very interesting to her. Whether this woman succeeds in her professed objective will depend on some factors beyond her control: Will her husband take a new job in another city or state? Will one of the children become embroiled in a crisis that demands her complete attention so that she drops school? But if she stays with it, she will make a fine teacher or a lawyer or perhaps someday a judge.

These loose sketches are drawn to disabuse some people of prevailing misconceptions about who and what community college students are. They are not Joe College of the fifties. Even less are they, typically, the hippies or radicals of the late sixties and early seventies. They are not dumb or lazy. And mostly they are not intellectuals. If they have a single trait in common it is probably a tendency to subscribe to and practice the old American belief in self-help through education and hard work. Considering the numbers of hours they must devote to jobs and families, in addition to full college loads, they are probably one of the hardest working group of students in the nation. Visit any community college campus and you will generally see relatively few students taking a leisurely stroll about the campus, listening to political speeches, or discussing Saturday's Big Game. The students move purposefully from class to class, and when their classes are over, they get in their cars and rush off—usually to a job. Even so, it should be pointed out that social activities and athletics abound on community college campuses, with numerous opportunities to participate in student government, clubs, and organized and informal student affairs.

The prevailing campus tone is not apt to be one of intense and abstract talk—although of course there is always some of that around for those who fancy it. Most of the talk is purposeful and immediately relevant, comparing and contrasting grades, instructors, and job opportunities, rather than metaphysical. Dress is casual and young, but not terribly far out. There is rarely any disorder, in class or out.

Sometimes a highly controversial speaker will be invited to the campus. Usually the problem is getting a crowd to attend. Those who do attend listen politely, ask a few questions, and sometimes go so far as to make known a disagreement with the speaker. Student newspapers sometimes get impassioned and controversial, but usually the principal demon of the community college press is student apathy—including the apathy of the students toward the press itself.

This is an attempt to draw an honest picture, including some characteristics that perhaps should be changed. A good many people, particularly among the humanities faculty, would be happier with this portrait if it included more intellectual passion and excitement. Also, the typical community college student is probably less involved with and concerned about the total college environment than one might hope for. Still, on balance, the picture is encouraging. It represents the dominant values of our society—individualism, hard work, order, courtesy, freedom to be different or not to be different—and, above all, openness, a willingness to listen, learn, and change.

It is by no means uncommon for community college faculty members to turn down attractive offers to teach at four-year colleges. Many abjure the title of professor—preferring to be addressed simply as Mr. or Mrs. or Miss or Ms. Even where professorial rank exists, it often is used to grant an additional annual stipend to a senior faculty member or to someone who has done some exceptional service, rather than a true system of academic hierarchy. Most community college instructors consider themselves fortunate not to have to engage in academic status-seeking. Many of them do extensive and important research and many are widely published. But this is commonly done for their own professional advancement and does not normally impinge on their primary responsibility to their students.

All things considered, most community college faculty members prefer the absence of pomp and circumstance and nonproliferation of meetings. Some of the younger ones doubtless regard a two-year college teaching assignment as a step on the path to a four-year institution. Some may wish to enter the ranks of administration. But the great majority tend to look on a two-year college teaching position as a career rather than as a step along the path of upward mobility, and have no more desire to teach in four-year institutions or to enter administration than, say, most small-town doctors wish to move to the big city or become heads of hospitals.

Perhaps one of the greatest positive attractions for the community college student and instructor alike is the generally informal and pleasant nature of the relationship between the two. High school teachers, unfortunately, are often forced into spending a disproportionate amount of time, energy, and thought in dealing with disciplinary problems, posed generally by a small minority of students who are in attendance solely because the law forces them to remain in school. University professors may appear to be somewhat awesome to a typical college freshman. In this regard community college faculty often have the best of both worlds. Because attendance is voluntary, disciplinary problems are rare on two-year college campuses. And few students tend to regard their instructors as educational grandees. The general tone, as at most institutions of higher education, is one of mutual respect, civility, and cooperation toward mutually desired ends. Most community college faculty members will readily testify that their work is generally pleasant and agreeable. Numerous studies of the attitudes of community college students about their instructors almost invariably reveal a high degree of satisfaction with their instructors' competence as scholars and teachers and with their accessibility. In short, faculty and students at these institutions usually like each other, and this fact alone often makes all the difference in the world.

Still, there are problems inherent in the nature of classroom teaching, problems largely responsible for the growth of the "publish or perish" syndrome in higher education. An instructor who teaches well is in the position of a doctor whose patients stay healthy. A student may go on to high honors and achievement, but his achievements reflect credit on his mentors only indirectly. Thus from time immemorial academics have sought devices for rewarding outstanding achievement in the classroom. Sometimes, however, the rewards in fact go to those who neglect the classroom in favor of pursuing the reward.

The problem is further complicated by the difficulty if not impossibility of measuring classroom effectiveness in an objective fashion. As almost anyone who has spent much time on a college campus will testify, some great instructors are very strict disciplinarians and hard graders. Others approach their subject very informally. A bromide of the public school administrator is that there is virtually no teacher so bad that some former student will not stand up at a public meeting and swear that this teacher was the inspiration of his life and directly responsible for saving many students from a life of crime. On the other hand, there is no teacher so good that someone will not be prepared to swear that this teacher is ignorant, biased, incompetent, and unfair. Teaching, like beauty, is often in the eye of the beholder.

In 1972 the Board of Governors of the California Community Colleges adopted a resolution requesting local colleges to set up objective criteria and procedures for periodic review of the effectiveness of classroom instruction. The board wisely left the matter of how this was to be accomplished in the hands of each college, with the stipulation that faculty members themselves be involved in the evaluative process. This is the beginning of a long process that ultimately aims at improving efficiency and recognizing superior dedication and achievement.

The fact is that although we know a great deal about the learning process, we do not know precisely how and under what circumstances all learning takes place. One student may sit quietly in the back of the room, taking no notes and appearing to be uninvolved. But five years later he may be able to tell you a great deal of what was important about that course. Another is constantly asking questions, raising points, and performing well on exams. Six months later he has forgotten almost everything, including the instructor's name. Why? We don't entirely know. We have a great many theories, generously supplied by half a dozen eminent schools of psychology. But the fact is that the experts disagree.

Until we have more precise knowledge of the process of learning, it behooves all of us to tread gently and cautiously in this realm. For there is real danger that good people will be harassed or professionally damaged. Physicians, with all their precise scientific training, are traditionally cautious about establishing criteria to measure another physician's performance. How much more complex is the challenge when the subject deals with the mind rather than the body.

With all these cautions firmly in mind, it is nonetheless necessary that an attempt be made to achieve a coherent and fair methodology for evaluating and improving classroom instruction. The stakes are too high, not merely in terms of dollars, but also in the vastly more important impact that the faculty must inevitably have in shaping the future, to leave such matters purely to chance.

There are now about 12,000 full-time faculty members in California Community Colleges. Their knowledge, skill, and dedication are the essential elements in a great success story. Effective leadership, sound policies, and adequate financing are necessary to make a college function. But in the last analysis much of what happens in education ultimately comes down to classroom instruction. And it seems self-evident, or at least should, that whatever the bureaucrats and politicians do in the state's capital, the endless discussion of policy, process, and budget, must ultimately serve to help students, or it accomplishes very little. For helping students is what education is about.

7

GOVERNANCE AND FINANCE

Before a community college can be a school, a community, a cultural and social asset, or a scholarly refuge, it must have land and buildings and instructors and workers—all of which require money. However high-minded an organization's stated goals may be, and however much the public may approve such goals, the test of whether institutions flourish or fail in this society often comes down to the question of whether they are able to generate sufficient income to meet their obligations. Only slightly less critical is the matter of how these institutions shall be organized and governed.

Thus power and money—or governance and finance, the less abrasive terms preferred by most educators—and how they are used go to the heart of most of the questions discussed earlier.

Traditionally, in most four-year colleges and universities, power and money have tended to flow from the top down: that is, *de jure* power to govern the college has resided in an appointed board of men and women, while *de facto* power has often resided in the senior members of the faculty. Money came either from wealthy donors—usually alumni, in the case of private colleges, or from the state or federal government—in the case of public institutions.

California's two-year colleges were organized and funded on a different basis. With their roots in the public school system rather than in higher education, it was natural that these institutions would take the prevailing patterns of local elementary and high school districts as a model for their own system of governance and finance. Thus local school boards were elected directly by the people, and funding came from local property taxes plus state subventions. At the time the original Master Plan for Higher Education was adopted in California in 1960, there appeared to be agreement on the principle of approximately equal support for the community colleges—that is, the state would pay 45 percent of the cost of these institutions, while local taxpayers and funds from the federal government would provide the balance. In point of fact, however, the state has never approached this level of funding. (Current statewide average of community college operating budgets is about one-third.)

Nevertheless, despite inadequate state support, most community colleges in California were, on the whole, in better financial shape until the great property-tax squeeze began in the mid-sixties. Until that time local taxpayers tended to respond rather positively to the appeal of local school boards for tax increases and bond issues needed to meet mushrooming enrollments in the community colleges. Then a number of factors, most of them not directly related to education, began to seriously affect funding. Rising welfare costs and rapidly expanding governmental services, many of them mandated by federal laws and court decisions, increased property taxes throughout California. Some people lost their homes or were forced to sell them because of inability to meet this growing tax burden. In many cases homeowners who, for a decade or more, had been making payments on 30-year mortgages saw their monthly tax payments rise above their original loan payments. "The power to tax is the power to destroy" is an axiom of government known since the time of the Romans. To many Californians, the property tax was threatening to destroy a cherished desire of the average family to own its own home. In the last half of the sixties and early seventies the voters, in simple self-defense, began to turn down even the most meritorious requests for school tax raises and new bonding proposals needed to accommodate growing enrollments.

The problem was further compounded by a trend in American society to extend the idea of equal educational opportunity into a growing belief that young people should not suffer an inferior education because they happened to live and attend school in an area relatively poor in available tax dollars. The California Supreme Court, in fact, ruled that existing inequalities in educational funding should be removed, although the precise terms and nature of that ruling and the response to it are still subjects of debate among state officials and educators. (One of the unanswered questions is whether the community colleges are included within the terms of the California court decision.)

In late 1972 the state legislature passed and Governor Ronald Reagan signed a bill which hopefully will remove at least some of the distress of local property taxpayers. The law does not directly affect community colleges—except that any measure which poses some relief for the harassed homeowner will be welcome by most community college people. The law also provides for new funding for the K-12 segment of education and makes a substantial contribution toward relieving a financial crisis for many local school districts in the state.

Similar relief for the community colleges appears to be in the offing. (A detailed and specific discussion of some of the problems of the community colleges can be found in the appendix.) At this point, and for the benefit of the general reader rather than for those whose business it is to concern themselves with the details of finance, the suggestion is reiterated that state funding of community colleges should be increased from the present state level of one-third to approximately one-half state and one-half combined local and federal funding. The logic of this remains what it has been for the past decade: the present level of state support is simply too low to do what must be done if the community colleges are to meet their stated objectives. On the other hand, state support far greater than 50 percent would probably be opposed by many California Community College people because it could pose the long-term possibility of greater state control, perhaps of total state control.

The question of increased funding inevitably leads to the other half of the equation with which this chapter began—how shall the money be spent and who shall decide?

For many years the concept of the locally elected school board has seemed to embody the essence of our democratic belief in the diffusion and decentralization of power. Recently new and sometimes strident voices have been heard to the effect that perhaps this idea is not really democratic enough, that there should be greater "participatory democracy." The idea that it might somehow be possible to return in some measure to the concept of a town-hall type of democracy in this complex and highly organized society may seem a bit farfetched. But clearly students, instructors, taxpayers—indeed just about everyone—seem less inclined to passively accept the decisions of constituted authority than in the past. There is a growing feeling that those whose lives are to be affected profoundly by a decision ought to have a voice in the decision-making process. Representative democracy provides that opportunity, of course, by way of the ballot box. But something more seems to be called for today. New forms and processes are being evolved to accommodate those who believe democracy implies not simply going to the ballot box every two or four years and choosing between men and parties, but also participating in the overall direction of those institutions.

Many local school boards in California have modified their procedures, both formally and informally, to meet this new situation. Others are in the process of doing so. Local boards—while retaining sole and exclusive decision-making power—are extremely well informed about student opinion, faculty opinion, and even the opinions of classified employees on a given matter of direct concern to these groups. Trustee meetings, traditionally businesslike affairs, tend to be a great deal livelier these days, with periodic outbursts of debate punctuating the normal discussion of regular matters of school business.

How far or deep this trend will run is difficult to guess. It seems safe to assume that the governance of the community colleges will continue to reflect prevailing tendencies in the larger society. As more and more people seek to become involved in decision-making in business, government, and labor, the same tendency will probably be felt and accommodated within higher education.

At the other end of the scale is the statewide Board of Governors of the California Community Colleges.

Prior to 1960 a nominal kind of authority was provided by the State Board of Education, charged with exercising some degree of leadership and disbursing state funds over a vast, loose educational empire that ran the gamut from kindergarten through state colleges, and which included the community colleges.

By 1960, when California adopted some provisions of the Master Plan for Higher Education, the State Colleges (now known as the California State University and Colleges) were separated from the State Board of Education, and the power to govern the system was vested in a statewide Board of Trustees created for that purpose. At the time some educators and political leaders felt that a similar pattern should have been established for the community colleges. However, many community college leaders were suspicious of what a state Community College Board might do to local control and hence preferred the status quo.

By 1967, however, the statewide Board of Governors of the California Community Colleges was established by law, and members of the board were appointed by the governor. Many community college leaders remained skeptical, fearing the beginning of the end of local autonomy. It is a tribute to the Board of Governors that although a healthy caution in respect to local control and the Board of Governors still exists, many of the early skeptics no longer feel any resultant loss of local autonomy whatsoever. The reason is that the state board has demonstrated that it is one of the most effective bulwarks *against* state control of the California Community Colleges.

The great strength of the community colleges lies in its boards of trustees, elected locally for four-year terms and accountable to the people of their communities. It is they who decide matters of college budgets, salaries, curriculum, and the gamut of local governance, management, and supervision. Each of California's 69 community college districts has five or seven trustees who are legally empowered to govern their district; some districts have one college while others are multicollege districts with up to eight campuses. This arrangement of state and local sharing of functions has worked well in California. And these delineated functions of local boards of trustees account for what is known in California as "local control."

In more than five years of operation, the Board of Governors has never made an important decision of statewide impact without first testing it against the touchstone of local control. The board sought and received, for example, legislation to return approval of individual classes to local boards of trustees and concentrate instead on approval of new educational programs, particularly as they affect more than one district.

In the area of personnel the board and the law have wisely left the matter of hiring and assignment of personnel to local management. Instead, the board has concentrated on streamlining the state credentialing operation, seeking and receiving legislation to make credential requirements simpler and less rigid and costly, leaving more decisions up to local boards, and reducing the cost of credentials to faculty and administrators. And the board continues to make changes in credential regulations to improve the procedures wherever possible.

Another clear distinction between state responsibility and local authority is in capital outlay needs and facilities planning. Although the state approves capital outlay needs for the community colleges, it does not attempt to initiate plans or to employ contractors to build the facilities. As a result, there is an understandable and acceptable delineation of functions between the state and the local districts; each knows where its responsibilities begin and end.

This clear delineation of functions between state and local operations is one of the most important ingredients in the success of the Board of Governors and, hence, in the success of the entire network of colleges. For, with very few exceptions, the community colleges, as a result, have been able to operate as a team, not as a system; as a family, not as a monolith—but also as a federation, not as completely disparate sovereignties and fiefdoms. While there is much to be done, it is remarkable that the Board of Governors has been able to develop educational positions that have ultimately been concurred in by virtually all elements and segments of the community colleges.

In all areas of community college life—finances, improvement of instruction, tenure, construction, program budgeting, districting, equal opportunities for disadvantaged and minority students, continuing and adult education, apprenticeship programs, occupational education, counseling and student personnel services, regulations for students transferring to four-year institutions—the Board of Governors has shown a mature sense of direction and innovation, as well as consultation and accommodation.

The new board has struggled with all these programs and problems, but its primary concern has inevitably been with an attempt to obtain adequate financing in a period of generally tight budgets and taxpayer resistance to rising costs. The past few years have seen large increases in enrollment without adequate financial means to accommodate the influx of students, while at the local level citizens in some areas decided that property taxes were too high and thus opposed any increase in this tax for any purpose, however worthy.

Enrollment increases in community colleges have been phenomenal. Since 1959, while the Master Plan for Higher Education was being developed, enrollment in California Community Colleges has increased about 180 percent. Since 1968, when the Board of Governors began operating, enrollment has increased over 30 percent. Indications are that enrollments have increased about twice as fast in the community colleges as in other segments of higher education, with about 850,000 students now in the community colleges and about one million expected by 1975.

The reasons for these enrollment increases are many. For one thing, the cost per student is low for the state—one of the lowest in the nation, in fact—and there are no tuition charges for resident community college students. As a result of this low cost per student, the state has encouraged the diversion of students from public four-year institutions to the state's two-year colleges. In addition, as tuition increased in private and public colleges and universities, more students were encouraged to attend community colleges.

Still another reason is that it became apparent at the end of the 1960s that the community colleges would provide the greatest opportunities for disadvantaged students. Not only were costs lower but, with far more campuses available, accessibility to a two-year college became a determining factor for economically disadvantaged students who could not readily travel great distances—and perhaps change jobs and move families—in order to go to college. In addition, although scores of community college students were scholastically eligible to attend a four-year institution if they wished, the fact that the community college open-door policy serves all students who can benefit from instruction encouraged still more students to enter college who otherwise might never have enrolled in a college at all.

Finally, the business slump and lower employment in the state in the late 1950s and early 1960s increased enrollments in the two-year colleges, which was no surprise to these institutions. The reason is that these are periods when many of the unemployed go back to be retrained for new technical jobs or professions, and when employed personnel more than ever go to community colleges to keep up with developments in their fields. Recently, for example, a number of unemployed engineers have been retrained by community colleges for technical employment.

At any rate, as a result of these confluences of increased enrollment patterns, many community colleges were filled beyond their capacities, and physical and financial constraints in recent years have been serious and critical.

President Richard Nixon in his Message to Congress in 1970 said that "A dollar spent on community colleges is probably spent as effectively as anywhere in the educational world." Governor Ronald Reagan in his State of the State Address in 1971 said that "our Community College system has no equal anywhere," and in 1972 stated that "we, in California, take great pride in our community colleges and in the fact that, in many instances, we have provided an example which other states have followed in creating their own systems. ...Our community colleges have been doing an exceptionally fine job of teaching.... There is increasing recognition by youth of the excellence of the education provided on the two-year campuses.... It is to the taxpayers' benefit that it would cost three times as much to educate the same students in four-year institutions." The community colleges are so important to the health of our society that financial changes must be made to protect the viability and quality of these two-year institutions.

8

THE CHANGES TO COME

Inevitably, the future of higher education in California will be shaped primarily by developments within the larger society, both in the state and in the nation, and one's estimate of that future will reflect one's diagnosis of America today. The past years of turmoil have demonstrated clearly and painfully the lack of wisdom in speculation about the future of education without recognizing the paramount importance of interaction between town and gown.

One has but to review the writing of educational futurists of scarcely a decade ago to realize how quickly and unpredictably things change. Almost all the great issues that have preoccupied educators for the past few years—the war resistance movement, attempts to integrate the campus fully, the acute financial squeeze, student rebellion and community disenchantment, drugs, the sexual revolution—were largely unforeseen by many of the state's and nation's leading educational seers of the early sixties. The Master Plan for Higher Education in California, for example, was concerned fundamentally, although not exclusively, with two issues—building new campuses and facilities to accommodate mushrooming student enrollment and attempting to achieve an acceptable delineation of functions for the three segments of public higher education in the state. These, of course, were the paramount issues of that time. Few educators today would put either of these questions at the very top of a current list of concerns.

Any effort to look to the future of California Community Colleges, based upon today's concerns, may seem shortsighted tomorrow. Nevertheless, unless we are content simply to drift with events, it is necessary for those who have responsibility to steer. And this involves some guesses as to the course ahead.

First of all, the current "youth revolution" in America—and through much of the western world—is probably symptomatic of profound changes in human and social values, rather than a transitory fad. For example, mass, inexpensive jet travel is breaking down rapidly the innocent provincialism once associated with youth, a trend that will undoubtedly be accelerated in the seventies. A recent poll of young people in America disclosed that one in three would like to live abroad for a year or more. Most large American corporations have become global in almost every phase of their operations. Millions of Americans are now working and living all over the world. Other millions travel abroad frequently. Thus, education that remains provincial and isolationist in outlook may simply be inadequate to the real needs of today's youth.

Although it was once reasonable for community colleges to train people only for local industries and business, the training now needs to be broadened. Furthermore, the new law giving 18-year-olds virtually full legal citizenship means that young people will be even more free to move about than in the recent past. Thus a young man who attends public school in, say, Los Angeles, may decide to attend a community college in San Francisco in preparation for a career that might take him to London or Tokyo. In the past this young man would have been required by law to attend his local college. Social and economic conditions could have kept him in the Los Angeles area. Neither condition obtains today. This means that those colleges located in attractive settings and boasting strong and specific occupationally oriented programs may experience greater growth than those that simply "service" local young people with traditional college courses.

The increasing sophistication of the young as the result of factors such as wider travel and greater exposure to the media will also require a concomitant upgrading of faculty. Instructors will have to know more if they are to hold the attention of their students. Marshall McLuhan has pointed out that if Huck Finn were created today, he would have to be about ten years old to be that innocent. In Mark Twain's day, Huck was a rakish thirteen or fourteen. Television, McLuhan points out, has destroyed adolescence in America. This may be a characteristic bit of hyperbole, but it contains an element of truth. Simply in terms of knowledge and experience with life—as well as in purely legal status—the 18-year-old American of today is a more complex and sophisticated human being than the 18-year-old was ten years ago. To keep up with these students, community colleges, primarily in entry level courses and material, will need to emulate the characters in *Through the Looking-Glass* who run as fast as they can in order to stand still.

For many decades Americans have been the supreme technicians of the modern world. We have led the world in adapting the insights of science to create unprecedented material abundance. Many of our most gifted young people have naturally been predominantly concerned with technology and its applications. The current generation, without sacrificing its technical competence, seems also to be taking a humanistic view of education. Today's young people want to learn how to earn a living, and they also want to learn how to make a full life. The young today seem to examine the concept of a career not simply in terms of a job, money, or status, but also frequently ask, "If I enter this field, what sort of environment will I have to live and work in? What will my relationships with other people be like? What sort of community and family life does this imply? Will there be time and opportunities for travel and leisure? Will the work provide continuing interest and challenge as well as security? What contribution to society will I be able to make?"

One suspects that in the not too distant future the era of educating a young person to become a competent nurse, technician, or engineer without concern for the wider implications of such education will be outmoded. Educators will have to rethink their offerings, not only in terms of teaching specific skills, but of an entire network of complex human and social relationships. The sharp line between vocation and avocation will become increasingly blurred. This does not imply that career-oriented education is likely to decline and that we are about to return to the classical English version of educating "the Gentleman." On the contrary, the career goal of the student is likely to become even more important than in the past, and educators will redefine vocation as preparation for a job and for a lifestyle. Thus, one contemporary labor researcher, Harold L. Shepard, found that younger workers ranked "salary" fifth in importance in job rewards most prized, below such factors as "interesting" and "authority to do the job."

As already noted, there are abundant signs that the extreme political militance that characterized college young people in recent years has already begun to take a more constructive turn. Students and faculty have emerged as a profound force in American political life, a force that will probably grow in strength and influence. The colleges have been politicized, if that term means not simply partisan militancy but an awareness of the fact that in the long run politics controls the life of the community and, hence, largely, the life of the individual. Those who are concerned about the quality and direction of that life must necessarily seek political influence. Politicians are becoming as eager to win the support of various academic groups, including student groups, as they now are to court the favor of a labor union or a large corporation. This seems likely to increase, if for no other reason, simply because of sheer weight of numbers.

After almost a century during which the dominant trend of American education was toward increasing centralization, there will probably be a move in the opposite direction. In this the California Community Colleges have a particularly important role to play. They have retained a large degree of autonomy in a time of strong recommendations for merger and consolidation. Preserving this local autonomy will require skilled and dedicated people in positions where the responsibility for making decisions lies. Each new problem or crisis could offer a fresh opportunity to restrict that freedom.

For example, after some disturbances in 1969 on college campuses in California—virtually none on community college campuses —legislation was introduced that would have established a statewide security force for California Community Colleges, run from the state Capitol. While some agreed with the objective of this legislation— greater campus security and an end to riotous disruption—the price to be paid for a statewide campus police force in community colleges was too high. A compromise was worked out: instead of establishing a statewide and hence mandatory security force, the legislation was modified to make it possible for those community colleges desiring such a force to acquire one, subject to control of local district authorities. Thus those who felt the need for tighter security were free to fulfill this need, and those who did not were not compelled to have on campus security forces under the direction of state authorities.

Similar vigilance will be required to protect local freedom in the years just ahead. The same social and psychological forces that seem to direct the flow of power from the community to the state and from the state to the nation could operate within the institution as well. While establishing and defending local freedom is not a new issue, the pressures to inhibit are strong. Extreme militance and acts of violence are invitations to repression. While there were few instances of bizarre behavior among community college faculty or students, the clamor for greater control by the authorities was directed primarily at the four-year institutions. But the two-year colleges are inevitably affected by the prevailing educational climate.

If academic responsibility—a useful term because at its core is the instructor's and the student's responsibility to search and to learn —is to be preserved, there will have to be self-discipline within faculty and student communities. The public will not and should not tolerate wanton destruction of property or physical terrorism on campus. The means to crush such behavior exists, and no one should doubt the willingness of the power structure to use its power when and if needed. On the other hand, appropriate restraint at the right time is necessary in order to discriminate between legitimate dissent, or harmless nonconforming behavior, and a real threat. The classic doctrine of a "clear and present danger" will need to be applied.

"Academic freedom" was relatively easy to establish and maintain in a time when its consequences for the entire community were less immediate and apparent. The obscure theories of an iconoclastic professor were of no great concern to the average citizen a few decades back. However, some years ago resistance to the Vietnam War, largely campus-based and led, brought into question the issue of the academy as a grave danger to society. And the issue was compounded by nonconforming dress and speech and student use of drugs. Hopefully, sometime soon the Vietnam War will have come to an end. The dangers of drug abuse should become apparent to anyone bright enough to enroll in college. Some of the extreme forms of behavior will have lost their novelty and their power to shock, and hence most of their charm. In other words, there are reasonable grounds for optimism that the decade will see a lessening rather than an escalation of conflict between campus and community.

One of the central concerns of higher education in the past few years has been a crash effort to move so-called disadvantaged persons off the streets and into the mainstream of American life via the campuses. The California Community Colleges have been a conspicuous leader in this effort. That leadership is expected to continue and to develop new programs that will substantially increase the number of disadvantaged and minority group students on every campus in the state.

Recently there has developed within the ranks of higher education a point of view that takes an increasingly pessimistic view of the possibilities of achieving equality through education. What is most interesting about this view is that it tends to emanate from people of high repute on the faculties of such bastions of liberal thought as Harvard University. Writers like Professors Daniel Bell, Seymour Martin Lipset, James Q. Wilson, James Coleman, and Christopher Jencks have published books and articles based upon research indicating that what happens in the classroom is probably less important than family background, ethnic traditions, and economic status in the competitive struggle for success.[1] Thus, they conclude, education alone cannot substantially alter existing social inequalities. For years classroom instructors have insisted that the critical factors in predicting academic success for a given student are not fine buildings, books, or even outstanding teachers—it is the student's own home and neighborhood environment. Obviously, this is not to say that there are not many examples of outstanding success stories about individuals who managed to triumph over unfavorable origins, or an equal

---

[1]*Public Interest, Fall, 1972.*

number of cases of individuals who fail both in school and in society despite the most advantageous beginnings. But, on the whole, persons from homes where education is valued will have greater classroom success than those where education is not, regardless of other factors, such as the quality of the school and level of instruction. This fact comes as something less than a revelation to most working instructors.

The danger is that this truism will be used as an excuse for not trying. The promise of equality in American life has always meant, not equality of status or income or achievement for individuals or for groups, but equal opportunity. The fact that Professors Jencks and Coleman have realized that absolute equality, like absolute justice, can probably never be achieved by mortal men may well be irrelevant to our moral obligation to continue trying, within the limits of human fallibility, to provide equal opportunity for all.

Part of the difficulty rising from the thesis of Jencks, Coleman, and others lies in the very meaning of the word "equality." Legal equality of persons (before courts of law, for example) has always been implicit in the "one man–one vote" concept of democracy. On the other hand, there is no evidence to suggest that anything approaching a majority of Americans has ever believed in economic or social equality of status and reward—as opposed to equality of opportunity to compete for that status and those rewards. Much of the current gloom about the prospects for achieving "equality" through education seems to confuse these very different concepts. It is clearly outside the scope of the educator to achieve, or even attempt to achieve, a perfectly equal American society. It is just as clearly his legal and moral responsibility to do whatever he can to provide equal access and opportunity to the knowledge and skills necessary to compete within that society.

Translated into educational policy, this means that the community colleges must continue to improvise programs designed to attract and hold students—from whatever group—hitherto largely excluded from higher education.

With respect to an issue that has been so deeply and tragically a source of turmoil and conflict in America's past, it would not be wise to indulge in easy optimism. Still it is difficult to resist the purely objective indications that the worst may be behind us. The success of young Black, Brown, and other minority groups in recent years can hardly help but open a path for their younger brothers and sisters in the years ahead. Success, like failure, feeds on itself. The initial shock of cultural conflict between the predominantly middle-class students and instructors with the predominantly economically deprived minority students and instructors has been absorbed. The community colleges in California have modified their procedures and practices to accommodate the legitimate needs of disadvantaged groups, while the more extreme and sometimes self-defeating "nonnegotiable demands" have been resisted. There is, therefore, every reason to expect that the years ahead will be smoother and more productive for both groups. But again, in a matter where passion and ancient injustice play so large a part, it would be rash indeed to predict that nothing but sweetness and light lie ahead.

Heretofore this chapter has been concerned largely with what might be called the "foreign policy" of the community colleges—that is, their relationships with the other elements of society. It would be well now to turn to domestic concerns.

At the head of this list, most educators would be inclined to put the issue of funding. And it is true that community colleges, while delivering an excellent educational product in terms of both quantity and quality, have not been treated generously with state funding in return. Also, as has been said, 100 percent state support of the community colleges has an overwhelming drawback. Total state funding would inevitably mean total state control. State control would deprive community colleges of their salient and valued characteristics—flexibility, diversity, freedom to innovate, and close and continuing interaction with the communities they serve. It would, indeed, make the very name "community college" something of an anomaly. Therefore, while fully cognizant of the gravity of the financial squeeze, a less drastic solution is advocated, lest the remedy kill the patient as well as the disease.

Instead, what the California Community Colleges need is greater equalization, greater fairness in the distribution of dollars. Those that need the dollars most should get first preference in allocation procedures. The foundation program (that is, the basis for minimal support of the college) for financial support ideally should be at the same level as the average cost of educating a community college student. Or perhaps the foundation program should be replaced by some kind of percentage-equalizing technique.

Certainly, the foundation program has not been fully able to take care of variations in local ability. And the foundation program has not been able to equalize completely, perhaps because at present it is almost $300 less than the statewide average expenditure per student. In any event, the foundation program has almost always been too low in respect to the costs of education.

At the very least, the state share of support of community colleges should be increased from the present 34 percent to at least 45 percent, as recommended in the Master Plan for Higher Education. This increase could lessen the load on the property tax, put the state in a position where it is paying more of a fair share of support of community colleges, and still not endanger local control.

Some sort of percentage-equalizing technique should be considered seriously; that is, an allocation basis (projected or desirable cost per student) that would be determined ahead of time. Also, the state share of that basis could be fixed at a certain percentage and dollars per student.

First of all, this would provide improvement in state-level predictability. Fiscal decisions could be based on a realistic cost per student rather than a less meaningful foundation program basis. The state legislature could then select a desired percentage state-sharing as the basis for funding. This would be adjusted for differences in local wealth in each community college district, and the effect would be greater equalization in the distribution of state funds.

Another technique that has been suggested in recent years is a proposal to levy a statewide uniform tax on local property, to be collected and deposited in a special state-level fund. This uniform tax would be in lieu of all or part of the present tax levied by community college districts for operating purposes. There have been objections to the collection and transmission of local tax revenue to the state capital for reallocation to local districts, with fears that such revenue would soon be counted as part of the state's contribution to the support of community colleges, and concern that the state would begin to use subjective judgments in allocation of the revenue. The state should refrain from subjective determinations in the allocations of support funds. Because community colleges differ markedly in size and in the kinds of communities they serve and the nature of programs and courses these communities want, the objective formulas used in the allocation of support funds must be broad enough to include these considerations. It should be understood that, because of these differences, expenditures per student in each district will also differ if equal opportunities are to be provided throughout the state.

It would be both impractical and inefficient to make such program and budget determinations uniformly for all community college districts in California. Certainly, at the very least, the present finance system can be improved. The foundation program, if it is kept, should be increased to the average cost per student in the 69 community college districts in the state. Too, the foundation program might be able to be differentiated for additional factors that cause costs to be high or low—such as the mix of courses demanded by students, the size of the college, and the general socioeconomic characteristics of the community served by the college. In addition, consideration could well be given to providing financial incentives to promote occupational education.

The question of adequate funding does not, of course, exist on the institutional level alone. Students need help desperately. Clark Kerr's proposal to establish a universal parallel to the GI Bill should be endorsed, thereby granting educational benefits similar to those that have gone to millions of veterans since World War II. It is likely that sometime during the present decade the federal government may enact such legislation, and the total cost may not really be a great deal more than that of current programs providing assistance in one form or another. Present programs—while admirable in themselves—may really be discriminatory against the average middle-class family. The rich can afford to send their children to college without much strain. The poor, increasingly, receive assistance in one form or another. It is the middle-class family that must scrimp and save for years to send a son or daughter to college.

It may be that the educational stipend to students will be tied not only to academic qualifications but to some relatively few hours of work as well. There are very few communities in America that could not benefit from the efforts of college students doing socially useful jobs for ten hours or so each week. Very few students would find such an assignment a serious drain on their academic energy. This proposal has another major benefit: it would bring town and gown closer together. Young people would have a little sharper insight into the world of work, and the mature would be slightly less likely to regard the younger students as lazy and useless malcontents.

Also, the present state retirement law is somewhat self-defeating in that it tends to keep many instructors in the classroom for thirty years or more. The result is that local districts must pay top salaries to a disproportionate number of instructors. The instructors themselves are under economic pressure to stay on the job well past the time when they might feel inclined to retire. The median age of faculty members should be reduced, and the most effective and economic way to achieve this is by policies that encourage rather than discourage early retirement. The average instructor at the top of the salary schedule can be replaced by a younger person for about 60 to 70 percent of his salary. This fact should be kept in mind when computing tables for retirement.

In the area of academic programs, the Board of Governors of the California Community Colleges moved recently to reduce drastically the number of courses required by the state for graduation. Again, the regulations adopted were permissive rather than mandatory on local districts. The districts are free to establish any reasonable pattern they deem proper for graduation. However, by this action the Board of Governors hoped to set an example in moving toward an educational system far less encumbered by tradition and required courses than in the past. In general college students ought to assume more rather than less responsibility for their own education, and this includes the selection of courses needed to complete that education. Institutions awarding degrees should insist on a minimum standard of knowledge and performance in vital subjects, such as history and economics, and demonstrated performance in the student's major field of concentration. How the student elects to meet these requirements might very well be left to his own discretion to a much greater degree than in the past.

Resistance to the abolition of required courses has sometimes met with the opposition of some instructors of these subjects—partly perhaps out of a feeling that the importance of the subject they teach is being downgraded and partly perhaps out of fear that most of their students and hence their jobs may vanish. Both fears may be exaggerated. Experience indicates that in most cases when required courses are made optional, enrollment does not decline abruptly. In fact, most students elect to follow along in pretty much the established pattern, partly, no doubt, out of habit and partly because they agree with their instructors that these courses are important. However, the psychological difference between taking a course because the student feels it useful and taking the same course because it is mandated can be profound.

Another related issue is the question of grades. The present system of awarding letter grades is undoubtedly popular with many students and faculty members. For the student it provides a rough measure —the equivalent of wages he would get on the job—of success or failure. There is some security in a solid "B." For the instructor it provides a solid stimulus and—let's face the fact—a teaching tool. Neither of these benefits is to be dismissed lightly. Students do need the security of knowing how well they are progressing, and instructors often need all the help they can get. The trouble is that—as anyone who has closely compared academic achievement with the world of work, success on the job, or with competence in a given subject will testify—the whole business of grades is sometimes considered the ghost in the academic closet. For the fact is that there may be little or no meaning that can be attributed to grades beyond themselves. Doing well in college means the student is likely to continue to do well in college—and very little more. Getting "A's" in English does not mean that the student is necessarily a gifted or original writer or speaker or a discriminating reader. Getting "A's" in logic does not mean that he or she is reasonable; it simply means the student does well in courses in logic.

At the other end of the scale the whole concept of academic failure may be questioned. If a man or a woman sets out to become a stenographer or a plumber or an accountant and is demonstrably unsuccessful, he or she is simply terminated. The same thing could apply to college courses. Again, a given level of performance ought to be required. Students who fail to meet that level should try something else or try again later. What about the student who fails repeatedly at many courses? A college might reasonably require a certain number of successfully completed courses each year on pain of expulsion.

Again, one need not be in favor of that happy state of permissiveness that obtains in some societies where it may be possible to remain totally illiterate while obtaining a college degree. If anything, standards of academic performance should be raised, specifically with respect to the mastery of fundamentals such as written and spoken English, American history, and the fundamentals of the sciences, economics, and mathematics. However, the proliferation of mandated courses does not necessarily contribute to this goal.

There will probably be a stronger trend in education toward a gradual revision of the letter grade system and to limit required academic courses to those clearly required for entry into a given vocation. At the same time there may also be a movement toward something like an examination that will require all students to demonstrate a certain level of competence—in economics and history and in the knowledge of certain elementary principles of, say, language and the sciences—before being awarded a degree.

The prospective technician certainly should be strongly encouraged to take courses in economics, history, and social or physical sciences. But entry into his chosen profession should not be barred by any wholly irrelevant requirements.

Finally, as has been noted previously, a mood of pessimism has crept into recent comments of many scholars about the role and impact of higher education generally. Thus Stanford Professor of Education Lewis B. Mayhew notes that, "A counterrevolution concerning the nature, scope and values of higher education seems clearly in the making."[2] He goes on to cite numerous studies and historic tendencies adding up to an educational "backlash"— specifically aimed at the more egalitarian colleges, such as the community colleges.

"In the past," observes Professor Mayhew, "liberal intellectuals have tended to support such things as expansion of junior colleges on the ground that they conformed to an egalitarian ethos without really jeopardizing preferred positions within the intellectual establishment. During the past five years, however, previously excluded groups of people have been demanding not only entry to higher education but entry into preferred positions as well." This has led, he argues, to the "backlash" and to increasing efforts to "ascribe definite limits to those higher education will accommodate."

He may be correct. However, it should also be noted that "liberal intellectuals" (or conservative intellectuals, for that matter) did not create the community colleges. In California at least, the community colleges grew out of the demands of people for more knowledge and training, not out of educational theory. It is a fact that at first thousands, then tens of thousands, and now hundreds of thousands of individuals—under no compulsion but the desire to improve the quality of their own lives—show up to register at California's community college campuses each fall. And it is this fact that sustains and validates these institutions. It is the concrete achievement of former community college students in industry, the professions, business, and higher levels of academic endeavor that justifies the existence of community colleges and assures their continuing growth.

Thus while fashions may change with the ups or downs of the current academic mood, of economic trends, and of political developments, the California Community Colleges are built upon a foundation sufficiently real and solid to assure their long-range prospects in the face of all but the most catastrophic of social changes.

Much has been written about California's unique role as a kind

---

[2]LEWIS B. MAYHEW, "Jottings," *Change*, Nov. 1962.

of laboratory for the western world. New institutions and lifestyles seem to emerge in California as curiosities at first, only to be accepted gradually by the rest of the nation and often by much of the world. California's Community Colleges clearly fall into this general pattern. Lightly regarded for many years, particularly in the eastern United States, community colleges have spread rapidly across the nation. The nature of our socioeconomic system, the unique role of young people in almost any industrialized society today and the growing demand for higher education all seem to point up the fact that if community colleges did not already exist they would have to be invented.

Californians are fortunate in that they have gone down this trail earlier and with greater thoroughness than anywhere else in the world. Most of the early doubts about the quality of these institutions have been laid to rest; uncertainties about what a community college is and who it is for have almost all been resolved.

Our major problems, on the other hand, are largely those that beset the entire nation and therefore inevitably have their influence on the campus.

Educators may be too much prone to the rhetoric of Boundless Opportunity and Golden Tomorrows. Perhaps it is a carryover from the familiar themes of commencement day addresses, or perhaps it is the inevitable result of working with the young and the idealistic. Nevertheless, it is difficult to restrain optimism about the future of community colleges in California, in the nation, and indeed in the world. Between the public schools, struggling to cope with mass, compulsory enrollments, and the traditional four-year colleges, struggling to adapt an essentially elitist tradition to a democratic society, the community colleges seem to have found a practical and workable middle path.

APPENDIX

THE CALIFORNIA COMMUNITY COLLEGES

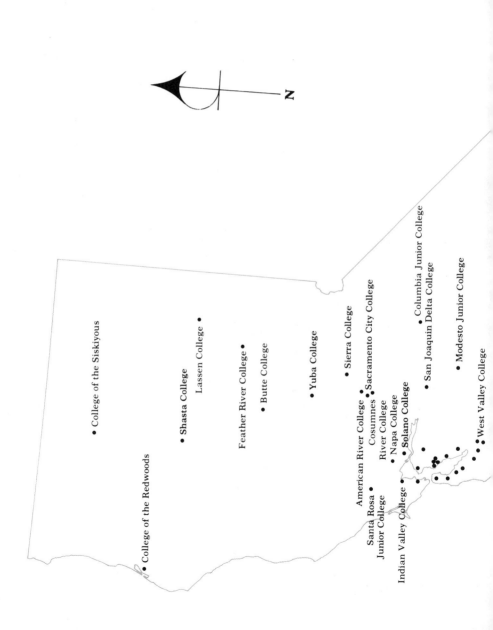

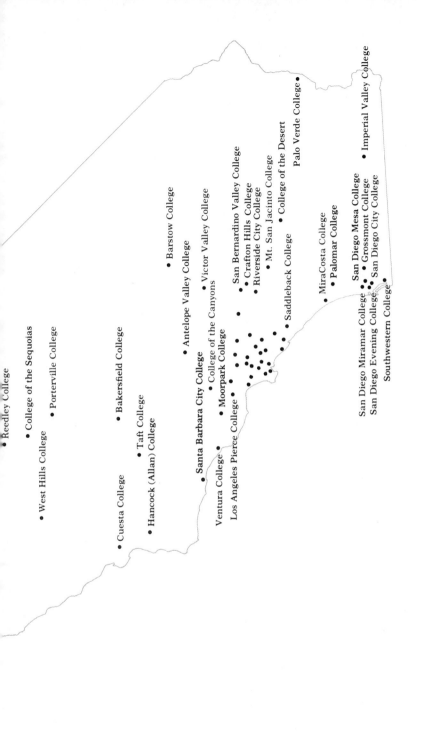

San Francisco Bay Area

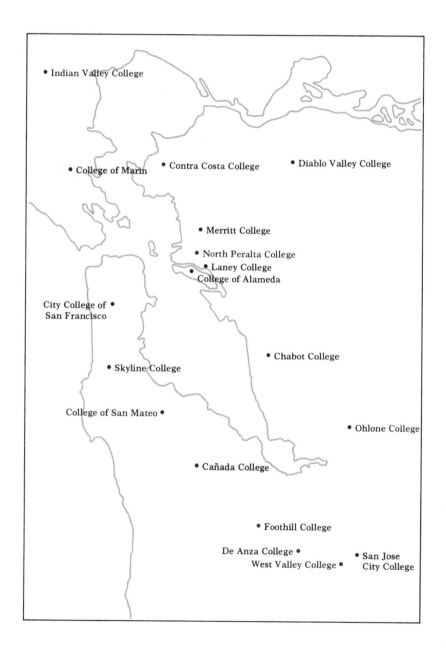

Los Angeles Area

• College of the Canyons

• Los Angeles Valley College

Los Angeles •
Pierce
College

Glendale College •

• Pasadena City College
Citrus College •

Chaffey College •

Los Angeles City College •

Santa Monica
City College •

West •
Los Angeles
College

• East Los Angeles College

• Los Angeles
Trade-Technical College

Rio Hondo College •

• Mt. San Antonio
College

Los Angeles Southwest College •

Compton College •

• Cerritos College

• Fullerton Junior College

El Camino College •

•
Long Beach City College

• Cypress Junior College

Los Angeles Harbor College •

• Santa Ana College

Golden West College •

• Orange Coast College

Saddleback College •

CALIFORNIA COMMUNITY COLLEGES, BY DATE OF FOUNDING

COLLEGE	STARTED	COLLEGE	STARTED
Fresno	1910	Monterey Peninsula	1947
Bakersfield	1913	Palo Verde	1947
Fullerton	1913	Orange Coast	1948
San Diego City	1914	Los Angeles Harbor	1949
San Diego Evening	1914	Los Angeles Trade Tech	1949
San Diego Mesa	1914	Los Angeles Valley	1949
Citrus	1915	Contra Costa	1950
Santa Ana	1915	Diablo Valley	1950
Chaffey	1916	Shasta	1950
Riverside	1916	Laney	1953
Sacramento	1916	Merritt	1953
Santa Rosa	1918	American River	1955
Gavilan	1919	Cerritos	1956
Allan Hancock	1920	Siskiyous	1957
Hartnell	1920	Foothill	1958
Modesto	1921	Cabrillo	1959
San Jose	1921	Barstow	1960
Imperial Valley	1922	Chabot	1961
San Mateo	1922	Grossmont	1961
Taft	1922	Southwestern	1961
Pasadena City	1924	Victor Valley	1961
Lassen	1925	Desert	1962
Ventura	1925	Merced	1963
Marin	1926	Mt. San Jacinto	1963
Reedley	1926	Rio Hondo	1963
San Bernardino Valley	1926	Cuesta	1964
Sequoias	1926	West Valley	1964
Compton	1927	Redwoods	1965
Glendale	1927	Cypress	1966
Long Beach	1927	Golden West	1966
Yuba	1927	DeAnza	1967
Porterville	1927	Ohlone	1967
Santa Monica	1929	Moorpark	1967
Los Angeles City	1929	Los Angeles Southwest	1967
Anetlope Valley	1929	Alameda	1968
West Hills	1932	Cañada	1968
Mira Costa	1934	Columbia	1968
San Francisco	1935	Feather River	1968
San Joaquin Delta	1935	Saddleback	1968
Sierra	1936	Butte	1968
Napa	1942	Canyons	1969
East Los Angeles	1945	San Diego Miramar	1969
Palomar	1945	Skyline	1969
Solano	1945	West Los Angeles	1969
Mt. San Antonio	1945	Cosumnes River	1970
Santa Barbara	1945	Indian Valley	1971
El Camino	1947	North Peralta	1971
Los Angeles Pierce	1947	Crafton Hills	1972

CALIFORNIA COMMUNITY COLLEGES, ENROLLMENT BY COLLEGE, SPRING 1972

COLLEGE	GRADED ENROLLMENT	COLLEGE	GRADED ENROLLMENT
Long Beach City	21,125	Marin	6,159
El Camino	20,286	Cañada	6,139
San Francisco City	19,567	Santa Barbara City	6,063
Orange Coast	18,806	Glendale	5,818
Los Angeles City	17,701	DeAnza	5,686
Los Angeles Valley	17,329	Merced	5,588
Los Angeles Pierce	15,417	Merritt	5,546
Los Angeles Trade Tech	15,391	Foothill	5,283
Pasadena City	15,169	Yuba	5,075
Mt. San Antonio	14,367	Sklyine	4,921
Fullerton	14,216	Sequoias	4,851
Diablo Valley	13,923	Cabrillo	4,730
San Bernardino Valley	13,834	West Los Angeles	4,583
East Los Angeles	13,786	Redwoods	4,564
San Mateo	13,214	Alameda	4,515
San Diego Evening	12,713	Sierra	4,404
Santa Monica City	12,316	San Diego City	4,397
West Valley	12,115	Antelope Valley	3,933
San Joaquin Delta	12,099	Ohlone	3,902
Grossmont	11,801	Monterey Peninsula	3,683
Chabot	11,458	Cuesta	3,650
Golden West	11,341	Los Angeles Southwest	3,620
Rio Hondo	10,842	Desert	3,588
Bakersfield	10,758	Napa	3,442
Riverside	10,527	Saddleback	3,316
Santa Rosa	10,309	Imperial Valley	2,974
Laney	9,889	Hartnell	2,633
Santa Ana	9,521	Butte	2,583
Modesto	9,196	Victor Valley	2,290
Cerritos	9,045	Cosumnes River	2,153
American River	8,888	Lassen	1,789
Los Angeles Harbor	8,530	Reedley	1,780
Ventura	8,501	Columbia	1,664
Southwestern	7,914	North Peralta	1,663
Citrus	7,856	Gavilan	1,644
Sacramento City	7,733	Mt. San Jacinto	1,585
Contra Costa	7,446	Canyons	1,505
Chaffey	7,336	Porterville	1,496
Fresno City	7,094	Mira Costa	1,381
Cypress	6,996	Barstow	1,202
San Diego Mesa	6,936	Siskiyous	922
Allan Hancock	6,665	West Hills	702
Moorpark	6,476	San Diego Miramar	583
Palomar	6,468	Feather River	556
Compton	6,358	Palo Verde	549
Shasta	6,267	Indian Valley	416
San Jose City	6,231	Taft	407
Solano	6,219	Crafton Hills	0
		Total	687,908

FINANCING OF
CALIFORNIA COMMUNITY COLLEGES

FINANCING OF THE CALIFORNIA Community Colleges is somewhat complex, depending on numbers of resident students, non-district students, out-of-state students, and adults. Essentially, community colleges receive state support on the basis of a district's assessed valuation per student and the number of students enrolled. Districts receive $125 basic aid (a basic grant) per student, with increasing amounts of equalization support going to poorer districts. On a statewide average the state pays for about one-third of the operating costs of community colleges; the rest is primarily paid from local property taxes, with a small percentage (about 6 percent) coming from federal funds.

This is essentially the same formula used in California to finance elementary and high school districts. As a matter of fact, there is one School Fund into which all state funds flow for money for kindergarten through community college levels. The University of California and the California State University and Colleges, on the other hand, receive no local property-tax funding.

There has been an increasing number of questions raised of late about the wisdom of financing community colleges in the present complex fashion. Proposals have been made to fund the community colleges 100 percent from state funds. Individuals in community colleges uniformly believe that the present one-third state support level is far too low, throwing too heavy a load on local property-tax payers. On the other hand, community colleges have rejected proposals for 100 percent state support because of the certainty that the state would then impose centralized controls on the campuses.

A reasonable solution to this financial dilemma would be a rejection of both extremes—the present inequitable arrangement of the state paying only one-third of the bill, and the other extreme of the state paying the entire bill. Clearly, it would be difficult for the Board of Governors of the California Community Colleges to hold off demands for more power at the state level if the state were to provide 100 percent support. For the facts dictate that local control of the community colleges is dependent upon some degree of local financial support. This danger could perhaps be avoided without excessively burdening local taxpayers if the state were to provide a reasonable percentage of support for community colleges. (The Master Plan for Higher Education recommended 45 percent state support.)

The state has good reason to assume greater support for the community colleges because these 96 campuses represent a great bargain in the state for higher education opportunities. Actually, in real dollars the cost per student in community colleges has dropped significantly in the last two decades. In 1951–52 the cost was $406 per student. Converted to 1971–72 dollars, this is a per-student cost of $1,018. However, the cost per student in 1971–72 was $923, meaning, of course, that the "real" (price-adjusted) cost per student actually dropped $95 during that period of time. There are many reasons for this phenomenon, including tighter fiscal controls and greater efficiency, but by far the most important reason is the increasing student/faculty ratio in the community colleges, which some believe has gone up close to 40–1.

The need for a body like the Board of Governors to strike a balance between local and state interests can be illustrated by a piece of recent legislation (AB 2887 of 1971, now commonly known as the Priolo Act) which lowered the age of majority in California from 21 to 18. One of the results of the Priolo Act is that 18-year-olds may be able to establish residence in any community college district by meeting district requirements of proof of residence.

This new fact may someday make planning on the community college district level far more precarious than it already is, for with easier and greater mobility of students, it may be difficult to determine how many students to plan for. Generally speaking, students in metropolitan areas may begin moving to more rural environments, and coastal and ecologically inviting areas may begin receiving far more students than would otherwise have been the case.

Financially, this is a problem for both districts that lose students and districts that gain students. Districts that lose students face a direct financial loss, since these districts receive state dollars on the basis of average daily attendance. Ironically, as a district loses students, it therefore becomes "wealthier," and eventually could lose its equalization aid because it has greater assessed valuation per student and would receive less state aid for each student remaining.

On the other hand, a district that gains students may not be much better off. Since the average cost of educating a California Community College student is presently about $960, and the state provides only $679 for each additional student, one can say literally that, depending on the local tax rate, some districts lose money on every student they take in.

One of the major though unintentional results of the Priolo Act was to reduce funds going to community colleges because of the so-called "defined adult" statutes in community college financing provisions. Before the Priolo Act, a "defined adult" in the community colleges was a student 21 years or older taking fewer than 10 hours of classes. Since, with the exception of those statutes related to alcoholic beverages, veterans benefits, and Youth Authority, the Priolo Act changed "21 years of age" to "18 years of age," the defined-adult provisions in community colleges were also changed from 21 to 18. And since the foundation program for community colleges provided $643 for regular students and $520 for defined-adult students, passage of the Priolo Act meant that community colleges would be receiving at least $123 less for the equivalent of many 18-, 19- and 20-year-olds in class. The resultant statewide loss to the community colleges would have been about $26 million.[1]

Further, the Priolo Act threatened to cut off an additional $1.5 million to community colleges from previous out-of-district fees. The reason is that about 5 percent of the state, in terms of geography and population (amounting to $2.5 billion, or 4.2 percent of the total $60 billion statewide assessed valuation), is not in a community college district. Before the Priolo Act, non-district territories sending students to community college districts, about 3.4 percent of community college enrollments, were assessed the cost of instruction for those students, based upon the residences of those students in the non-district territories. After the Priolo Act, it would have been impossible to continue doing so, since those non-district 18-year-olds could now change their own residences at will.

In addition, lowering the age of majority from 21 to 18 meant that out-of-state 18-year-olds could now attend these colleges without paying out-of-state tuition, a loss of about $6 million to the community colleges. (Nonresident tuition in community colleges is $750 for the 1972–73 academic year and will increase to $810 in 1973–74.[2] And along with other problems the

---

[1]Subsequent legislation (AB 686 by Assemblyman Paul Priolo of Los Angeles County) has determined that "defined adults" in community colleges would not be affected by the Priolo Act.

[2]Subsequent legislation (AB 666 by Assemblyman Leroy Greene of Sacramento) made nonresident rules for community colleges the same as for the University of California and the State University and Colleges—one year in the state for tuition purposes.

Priolo Act meant a potential loss of $400,000 to community colleges under the handicapped program for "minor" students. Since there are relatively few students in these colleges under 18—handicapped or otherwise—the new age of majority virtually prevented them from receiving any of these funds.

The potential loss of about $33 million because of the Priolo Act meant that unless something were done many two-year colleges would have to reduce their faculty to compensate for the loss. And by California law, faculty have to be notified by March 15 of each year if they are not going to be rehired.

Therefore, the first response of the Board of Governors to the Priolo Act was to introduce on the first day of the 1972 legislative session a bill to delay until May 1, 1973, all statewide fiscal effects to the Act. Senate Bill 10 was introduced by Senator Fred Marler of Redding and coauthored by Senator Walter Stiern of Bakersfield. The Board of Governors asked for a two-thirds vote in the legislature so that the bill would become law on the day the governor signed it. The bill passed the legislature with no negative votes and was signed by the governor on March 14, 1972.

SB 10, of course, was only a partial solution to the problem. It took immediate pressure off the community colleges, permitted them to plan a year in advance, and gave them time to develop substantive legislation for permanent corrections to the Priolo Act.

In respect to non-district territories, the long-run solution to that problem is, of course, to insure that all areas of the state are in a community college district. To accomplish this, the Board of Governors introduced legislation, which has been signed into law, requiring all non-district territory to be in a community college district by September 15, 1975, or else face the prospect of the Board of Governors mandating those territories into a district.

California Community Colleges, probably the largest segment of higher education in the free world, represent an enormous business enterprise—more than $565 million a year. Of this, about $339 million, or 60 percent, comes from local sources, about $192 million, or 34 percent, from the state, and about $34 million, or 6 percent, from federal sources. For capital outlay purposes, about $44 million will be spent in 1972-73 from a $160 million community college construction bond authorization approved by the voters in the November, 1972, general election. Local districts will supplement this amount by about $59 million, for a total capital outlay of $103 million.

There are approximately 12,500 full-time faculty and about 1,900 administrators in the California Community Colleges. Median salaries of faculty are about $11,000 the first year, $13,000 the 5th year, $15,000 the 10th year, and $18,000 the 15th year. In some districts faculty salaries go to a high of about $23,000. Enrollment in the California Community Colleges in 1971-72 was more than 825,000, with about 300,000 full-time and 525,000 part-time students. For purposes of fiscal allocation, this converts to about 590,000 average daily attendance in 1971-72. About 866,000 students are estimated to be enrolled in 1972-73. When community services are included, community colleges serve more than 1,000,000 people, or one out of every 20 Californians.

What is required to manage and protect the investment of such a large and important enterprise are some long needed changes in the financial structure of the California Community Colleges. Although they want to maintain a close relationship with the K-12 segment, along with other segments of education, community colleges are unique and important enough to consider whether someday they may wish to be funded in a way suited to their special role and function.

There should also be provisions for automatic cost-of-living adjustments for these colleges. To expect local property-tax payers to take up this slack each year because the state does not keep up with inflationary costs in the community colleges is unreasonable.

Further, community colleges may wish to consider being funded through a formula based on actual or anticipated cost per student. Such a program should also be based on prices that community colleges need to pay for necessary resources and the student-discipline mix. That is, since some disciplines are more expensive to teach than others, with different maximum numbers of students in classes and in the program, these factors should be considered in any changes in financing patterns. In addition, the allocation basis should also be predicated on new programs, changes in local tax base, and district size. There might also be a joint-powers tax for special regional ventures, to encourage districts to continue and accelerate development of joint programs across district lines. And to give this proposal the full support needed to operate it there should also be state dollars set aside to add to this joint-powers tax to stimulate programs by two or more districts. At the same time an equalization formula would have to be developed, as well as a formula to insure distribution of dollars on an objective basis in keeping with a district's ability. In addition, consideration should be given to ways of providing fiscal incentives to community colleges for occupational education.

These proposals, added to a built-in annual adjustment for inflationary state and local costs, based on a consumer price index, are the minimum changes to be considered for community college financing. At any rate, it is imperative that these two-year colleges have the kind of financing structure needed to insure high quality education for so many of California's citizens.

A financial unknown facing the California Community Colleges is the famous *Serrano* v. *Priest* decision, rendered by the California Supreme Court in a class action for school children in Los Angeles County, that the current method of school financing in California is unconstitutional. The suit was initially dismissed by the trial court and although the dismissal was upheld by the court of appeal, the California Supreme Court held for the plaintiff. The *Serrano* v. *Priest* decision holds that the present system of financing public schools in California is unequal and unfair. The decision does not rule out the present use of local property-tax dollars to fund public schools, but specifies that each district should be able to get equal educational opportunities for its students from similar tax efforts. Districts choosing the same tax should be able to spend at the same level. A district could, if it wishes, use a lower tax rate and spend less. The ruling does not require uniform state spending or an equal amount of money spent for each student, nor does each district have to have the same quality of educational program. Assessed valuation would not have to be abolished as an educational tax base, nor would the state have to stop spending extra money for special educational needs or programs.

The question yet to be answered for community colleges is whether they are included in this ruling. The court declared the present finance system to be unequal and unfair because the range of wealth of California K-12 districts, based upon student/assessed valuation ratio, is 10,000 to 1. In community colleges, however, the range is far less, from about $357,000 assessed valuation per average daily attendance, or 9½ percent state support, to $42,000, or about 50 percent state support. Average assessed valuation per average daily attendance in the state is $130,000. It may be several years before decision and action on the *Serrano* v. *Priest* ruling are final, and, until that time community colleges may not know if they are included in the judgment.

STATEMENT TO THE CALIFORNIA LEGISLATURE'S JOINT COMMITTEE ON THE MASTER PLAN FOR HIGHER EDUCATION

Sidney W. Brossman, Chancellor
California Community Colleges

March 22, 1972

MR. CHAIRMAN, MEMBERS of the committee: I appreciate this opportunity to provide information concerning alternative forms of higher education. The California Community Colleges are offering a wide variety of forms of education to meet the needs of the total spectrum of society, and we thank you for making this area one of the major study topics in your research plan. In this statement I will address my remarks primarily to the questions listed by the Joint Committee in the Study Plan as they relate to Community Colleges....

I. The first question, concerning the need for new forms of higher education and possibly new types of higher institutions, points up the fact that the changing needs of our society actually require that we review periodically our existing institutions as part of an ongoing process.

Generally speaking, the institutions and segments of public higher education in California are sufficiently diverse and flexible to meet the needs of the people of California. The University of California is the primary state agency for research and has jurisdiction over doctoral programs and a number of graduate programs. The State University and Colleges have heavy emphasis upon upper division, teacher education, and many master's degree programs. Community Colleges are exclusively two-year institutions with academic transfer and occupational education programs on each campus. The Joint Committee may wish to consider whether these segmental functions should be sharpened to insure that each institution is as responsive as possible to changing needs of society.

Speaking specifically about Community Colleges, one of the most important functions of these institutions is to adapt readily to education and technological innovations. By concentrating on the first two years of college and by emphasizing counseling and teaching, the Community Colleges have developed and implemented a large number of innovations. Many new ideas being discussed in higher education today have already been in effect in the Community Colleges for a number of years.

California Community Colleges have been utilizing store fronts, classes "without walls," and auto-tutorial laboratories for some years. Self-paced programmed instruction with audio and visual methods and equipment is being used at Pasadena City College in dental assisting and nursing education. Columbia College and American River College have such programs in natural sciences. Mount San Jacinto College and the College of San Mateo have instituted these programs in nursing, typing and bookkeeping. Skyline College has bilingual labs. Foothill College and San Jose City College have joint programs geared to special needs of disadvantaged students. Golden West College has developed such labs in several fields, including remedial English. In biology labs audio tapes are used to advise students how to conduct experiments with equipment. Paraprofessional aides maintain the laboratory and are available to assist students.

California Community Colleges are also using computer-assisted instruction with terminals disbursed among some of the campuses to provide students with access to large numbers of programs and learning sequences. Also in use are multi-media centers and classrooms, instructional television, cooperative education, including various forms of work experience at the sites of employers, store fronts, satellites and other off-campus learning centers, mobile advisement centers and mobile classrooms, short courses incorporating residential week ends, and concurrent enrollments.

II.   A number of alternative delivery systems of higher education should be developed, or at least tried, in California; some of them are already in operation in the Community Colleges. Computer-assisted instruction should be expanded for use by as many departments on campus as appropriate. These programs should be used to supplement regular course offerings, for terminals are now able to display graphs, pictures and text. Future innovations could include audio responses from the equipment to shorten the interaction time now required by typing responses.

Multi-media centers and classrooms have become common throughout the California Community Colleges. Permanent installations are now being used with more reliable and flexible equipment. Several Community Colleges, such as Chabot, Solano, Cañada, and Skyline, have planned and provided the necessary wiring in new facilities for equipment which is to be installed at some future time.

A.   The "university without walls" concept should be encouraged in California by the existing segments and in existing institutions.

In this connection, the California Community Colleges are using instructional television more and more extensively to break out of the traditional mold of the classroom. San Bernardino Valley College has been a pioneer in instructional television and, for example, regularly produces programs for elementary school districts. In addition, 22 Community Colleges in the Los Angeles area now participate in a consortium. The College of San Mateo produces programs for a consortium of Community Colleges in the Bay area. Golden West College also has production facilities. More than 31,000 persons have taken advantage of courses presented by Community College television. The Joint Committee should consider ways of encouraging the expansion of this method of teaching.

At least as important as production of programs over commercial and educational channels is the use of closed circuit TV. Two modes are in use in Community Colleges: (1) video tapes of carefully produced programming are piped on order from the campus TV center to the classroom, and (2) TV cameras, monitors and video tape recorders are used in the context of the classroom. Instant replay features allow students to view themselves and are proving to be effective particularly in a variety of training situations.

B.   Off-campus learning centers should be developed as supplements to existing institutions of higher education. Higher education must deliver education more effectively and deliver it where the people are, rather than merely where the campuses exist. California Community Colleges have been using off-campus learning centers as a way to reach California citizens where they live and work. Store fronts, satellites, and other off-campus learning centers have been developed experimentally by the Peralta Community College District with assistance from the Office of Economic Opportunity and have been developed by Merced College with assistance from the Higher Education Act, Title I. City College of San Francisco is currently planning off-campus learning centers located in ethnic neighborhoods.

Mobile advisement centers are also operated by many Community Colleges, after pioneering programs were started by Los Angeles City College and Contra Costa College. Mobile classrooms are used extensively in a major Manpower Development and Training program by Community Colleges in San Bernardino and Riverside Counties. The programs are brought physically to target groups of students.

Short courses incorporating residential weekends or other concentrated blocks of time are also becoming more common as the Community Colleges become more responsive to the needs and constraints of various career and community groups. Intensive semesters are in the planning stages at Community Colleges for programs where packets of books and instructional materials are sent to registered students eight weeks in advance of a seven-day, full-time "semester." After this intensive learning experience, the student has six to eight weeks to prepare reports on his own time before a final follow-up and testing session on campus. Many variations are possible. Cabrillo College is currently conducting an experimental program in which a one-month winter "semester" is offered between two four-month semesters. This enables students to earn quickly up to six units of credit by taking two needed classes and to keep pace if they have failed one or two subjects during one of the four-month semesters.

III.   Apprenticeship programs and community service play important roles in the learning process. The California Community Colleges have perhaps the most extensive apprenticeship and community service programs of any segment of higher education, public or private, in the state and perhaps in the nation. Many of these activities are as important as any that take place in higher education, including formal classroom settings and should, therefore, be recognized as a part of higher education.

An apprenticeable occupation in the Community Colleges is one which requires independent judgment in the application of manual skills and knowledge. It is best learned through an organized system of on-the-job training together with related and supplemental instruction.

There are over 400,000 students enrolled in occupational programs in the Community Colleges. Apprentices represent about 4 percent (15,000 students) of those enrollments. These programs are conducted in 48 Community Colleges and include 62 percent of all apprentices in public education and more than 50 percent of all California apprenticeship classes. In most instances, apprentices are part-time students and attend evening classes.

Although apprentices represent a relatively small percentage of students in occupational education in the Community Colleges, apprenticeship programs fill an important need in our economy. Unique to the apprenticeship program is on-the-job training and related instruction in cooperation with employers and unions.

This kind of cooperation has also resulted in strong community support for other occupational programs. Many students have continued with college work beyond the apprenticeship program and might never have participated in occupational education at all if it were not for the existence of apprenticeship programs.

More than 70 percent of the Community Colleges maintain programs in community services. These services include those educational, cultural and recreational programs of the college which meet the needs of the community beyond the normal confines of the college instructional program. These are directed toward providing leadership and facilities for the needs of individual communities.

Community services represent one of the major functions of the Community Colleges and are fully supported by local districts without any financial aid from the state. The colleges use their buildings, grounds, libraries, and other facilities for public, scientific, literary, educational, recreational and other public organization meetings concerned with the general enrichment of the objectives of citizens of the state. Examples of community service programs include such activities as community forums, institutes, conferences, lectures, community development meetings, films, music and theater programs, planetariums and museums, seminars and other meetings. These types of informal learning alternatives are becoming more and more well attended by the citizens of Community College districts and should be encouraged. They provide learning opportunities for citizens of the community of all ages and all levels of education.

IV.   Continuing education and retraining are critically needed in California, and the California Community Colleges are maintaining and expanding their function in this important role. Very often the only direct contribution of higher education to the citizens and taxpayers of this state is through adult and continuing education, a function for which all of California depends upon the Community Colleges. The Community College role in continuing education should be expanded, not curtailed, for California has a deep interest and concern in the mobility and strength of Community College continuing education, and I urge the Joint Committee to consider ways of strengthening the Community College role in this important area of citizen education.

Any decline in the overall economy of the state, any decline in employment, and any redirection in industry and technology—such as in engineering—results in increased dependence upon the Community Colleges for retraining education. Today the Community Colleges are playing a major role in retraining persons for employable fields, and the beneficiaries of this concentrated service are the citizens, taxpayers, and all of society in the state.

Alternative delivery systems to meet these needs are constantly required. The Community Colleges, for example, are developing regional planning for higher education in Northeastern California. This planning has been explored by eight colleges serving this region, and a Special Opportunity Grant has been approved for this purpose. The Office of Economic Opportunity program facilitated the initial explorations and participated in a series of planning meetings. The grant seeks to assess needs for higher education in the Northeastern rural, economically depressed region, to develop programs to meet these needs on a regional basis, and to plan the construction and use of facilities necessary to deliver the new educational services. Three primary areas of activities are projected:

1.   Offering baccalaureate degree programs of Chico State College and UC Davis at the six Community College campuses as part of their new extended degree programs. Certain degrees can then be obtained by part-time students without meeting old-fashioned residency and admissions requirements, and the special hardship of long-distance travel in this rural region is overcome.

2.   Career education programs will be planned in accordance with regional manpower planning and the special resources of each segment of higher education. Community Colleges will develop new associate arts degree curricula incorporating the in-service training needs of major employers and updated concepts of core curricula, such as Butte College and Yuba College are doing with the Migrant Education program and Elementary and Secondary Education Act programs in those two counties. Chico State and UC Davis will assist the joint planning and commit themselves to the development of new upper division curricula to meet the needs of students with associate arts degrees whose backgrounds emphasize work experience and occupational training. An early childhood development program, for example, is being planned involving Shasta College, Chico State, and Shasta County.

3.   The development of innovative delivery systems and facilities will derive from the needs assessment and program development phases of the Special Opportunity Grant study. Community Colleges have developed such alternatives as the use of mobile advisement centers, carrying counseling and resource referral services to rural sites, in combination with "intensive semesters," which bring rural students on campus for several consecutive days in residence after a period of self-study or programmed instruction. Other alternatives include new methods of using educational TV or video tape and the construction of a regional residential adult learning center. Community Colleges were key facilitators in the various planning sessions that resulted in the Special Opportunity Grant program.

V.   Existing institutions of higher education should consider modifying degree requirements so that degrees may be offered to individuals who have acquired skills and knowledge through experience and self-education. It should not be necessary to create special mechanisms or agencies to do this.

Cooperative education including various forms of work experience at the sites of major employers in industry is now common practice in career education programs in the California Community Colleges. The College of San Mateo, in particular, has implemented the concept successfully. The Antioch Plan of alternating semesters of work and study is also currently being considered by some Community Colleges. Core curricula are also being developed in several career education fields. San Diego City College, Mesa College, Grossmont College and Southwestern College are currently working with San Diego State College and the UC Medical School in San Diego to develop core curricula in health which will serve students in a variety of allied health professions. Gavilan College has developed a general education core to assure that, within their very limited resources, students get an integrated exposure to the academic disciplines.

Recently the Board of Governors of the California Community Colleges revised Title 5 of the Administrative Code to remove mandated courses for the associate arts degree. The reason for this action was to give local boards of trustees maximum latitude in revision of requirements for degrees, including consideration of experience and self-education. Certainly there is much that higher education can do to consider experience and self-education as part of the requirements for college degrees. Increased challenging of courses so that students can demonstrate the efficacy and relevance of their experience and self-education should be considered by all segments of higher education.

Pilot programs in the Community Colleges involve major employers of paraprofessionals in education, such as the Migrant Education program, school districts with Elementary and Secondary Education Act programs, and Model Cities having Career Opportunity Programs. Community people are employed in Community Colleges as aides in learning situations for disadvantaged where they are already familiar with the cultural background of the students and can serve as realistic role models. The employers, local Community Colleges, and nearest four-year schools of education enter into a joint planning venture which meets in-service training needs of the paraprofessionals and develops curriculum leading to the AA degree at the Community College with appropriate credit for the student's work experience and in-service training. The AA degree becomes the foundation for the new upper division curricula leading to the BA and teaching credentials at the four-year college. Professional education credit is granted for specified lower division work, and practice teaching is revised into increments some of which are met by work experience portions of the AA degree program. The four-year school of education develops a consultancy relationship with both the employing agency and the Community Colleges, including limited responsibility for supervising work experience. The Joint Committee should consider revising the Education Code in order to update the Code with successful practices being documented in these pilot programs.

VI.   While traditional campuses may for some time continue to be the primary higher education delivery system in California, they should not constitute the exclusive delivery system. It's possible for the present traditional campuses to become more innovative in the programs they provide.

Concurrent enrollment as operated by Merritt College is an example of an effective educational innovation. This program provides opportunity for Community College students to enroll concurrently in nearby four-year institutions. These students, with ability to do the work but with low motivation in their backgrounds, are helped with concurrent enrollment to overcome problems of transition of Community College students moving on to upper division studies. Merritt's program has demonstrated that, as fully matriculated students, they're much better prepared to make the transition without problems they might otherwise have encountered.

Experimental colleges have also been started on some Community College campuses. There seems to be two patterns. In both, students suggest courses. In one pattern the college supplies credentialed instructors, approves the courses and gives credit for them. In the other the college supplies rooms and an instructor for part of his scheduled teaching time. In both, if the course attracts enough students and has appropriate content, it is made part of the regular curriculum. Another innovation is the use of modules in subjects, allowing students to challenge any module and then studying those they are not familiar with. A different innovation is the use of contracts which allows a student to study full time on one subject for a short period and then take the examinations. After completion he goes to another contract.

Much can be done with the off-campus centers, satellites, and store fronts discussed earlier in this statement. But a great deal can also be done by improving on the delivery system of the traditional campuses themselves. The California Community Colleges have initiated a series of preplanning meetings with representatives from Compensatory Education in the State Department of Education, the Migrant Education Program, and with Yuba College, Butte College, Chico State College, and Butte County. Planning is under way using approximately 200 aides employed by Migrant Education Region II as the pilot group to be supplemented by 60–70 Elementary and Secondary Education Act aides employed in Butte County. The total education program involves new in-service training for classroom teachers and others besides the aides. The Migrant Education staff are ready to utilize this approach and plan equivalent programs in each of their other regions in California. A separate program is currently being developed by Chico State, Sacramento State, and several Community Colleges in early childhood development to meet the needs of the child care centers sponsored by Migrant Education. Preplanning meetings have also been held with Shasta Community Action Program regarding the Headstart Program it sponsors. We anticipate that their needs will fit into the emerging pilot in early childhood development.

The Community Colleges have also met in several sessions with directors and key staff of Model Cities in Richmond, Berkeley, and Oakland regarding joint development of an urban counterpart to the Migrant Education program. Aides in the Career Opportunities Program are the initial target group, to be supplemented by other Elementary and Scondary Education Act aides working in the same schools. Community Colleges to be involved are Contra Costa College and Laney College, with the possible addition of Merritt College, Alameda College and Chabot College. Hawyard State College and UC Berkeley will be approached, and San Francisco State's School of Education has already expressed interest.

VII.   Alternative forms of higher education should be evaluated on the basis of effectiveness and ready availability of higher education for students. Alternative forms should be used if they provide the kinds and forms of education and programs students need to find employment and to become productive citizens in society. Alternative forms should provide for cooperation and sharing among the segments of higher education. Alternative forms should bring educational governance closer to the people of California and thus provide the kind of decentralization and diversity that will increase the quality of higher education with prudent expenditure of public funds.

The use of alternative forms of higher education in California on these bases will also do much to heighten public confidence in educational institutions, and I urge the Joint Committee to consider these kinds of changes in higher education in the state.

CALIFORNIA COMMUNITY COLLEGES ANNUAL OCCUPATIONAL EDUCATION REPORT, 1971–72

POSTSECONDARY VOCATIONAL EDUCATION

According to long-standing tradition, the greater part of postsecondary vocational education in California has been offered in the Community Colleges. By state law, one of the principal purposes of the Community Colleges has been to provide vocational training. The other purposes have been (1) to offer courses for those planning to transfer to four-year instItutions of higher education and (2) to provide general education courses for cultural, recreational, or civic purposes.

Occupational education in the Community Colleges has been planned to provide the knowledge and skills needed by a student to obtain a job and to advance. This objective has been carried out through short-term certification programs, apprenticeship education, two-year occupational programs leading to an associate of arts degree, and courses designed to upgrade employment and to lead to job advancement.

Vocational training has been so combined with the other purposes of the Community College that the students pursuing vocational education objectives have been indistinguishable from students pursuing transfer programs or general programs.

The importance of postsecondary vocational education to the Community Colleges is clear when it is realized that of the total 1971–72 enrollment of 851,834, more than 63 percent (539,359) of the enrollees pursued some occupational training goal. Approximately 35 percent of the students were engaged in transfer programs (6 percent of the students were expected to transfer to a four-year college or university during the year), and the remainder obtained general education benefits.

There are 94 Community College campuses located throughout the state and concentrated in metropolitan areas (San Francisco Bay area—18; Los Angeles area—24; San Diego area—7). The Community Colleges in California comprise the world's largest system of higher education.

Occupational education in the Community Colleges is grouped in ten general areas. Accomplishments in each area is discussed as follows:

Agricultural Education

The field of vocational agriculture was served by 40 Community Colleges, an increase of three over the past year. One hundred and fifty full-time instructional staff members served 12,846 enrollments.

A curriculum guide for power equipment instruction in Community Colleges was developed in cooperation with West Hills Community College. This publication was in keeping with the continuing trend toward increasing the number and quality of power equipment instructional programs.

In-service workshop sessions were conducted for Community College agricultural instructors in hydraulic and diesel maintenance and trouble-shooting.

Distributive and Office Occupations Education

Distributive education enrollments increased in the past year from 43,164 to a total of 55,811, and office occupations education enrollments increased from 131,594 to 184,555.

Accounting Education Workshop   Educators and CPA practitioners met recently to discuss accounting education in Community Colleges. The California CPA Foundation for Education and Research, in cooperation with the Chancellor's Office of the California Community Colleges, hosted a two-day workshop in Palo Alto in February, 1972. Representatives from 12 Community College districts throughout the state met with representatives of several four-year colleges and members of the CPA profession to (1) discuss the Foundation's study, "Accounting Education in California Community Colleges," (2) identify and discuss the role of the Community College in accounting education, and (3) learn of the work of the California CPA Foundation, in order to establish closer relations and understanding between the accounting profession and the accounting educators. This represents a significant step in a meaningful articulation between the CPA profession and the Community Colleges.

Banking and Finance Program   The third year efforts regarding the California-American Institute of Banking Board of Directors (CAIBBOD)/California Community Colleges joint efforts in designing and implementing the AIB Banking and Finance Programs in Community Colleges of California proved to be most productive. With CAIBBOD appointing two permanent staff members to devote full-time energies to this assignment, the consideration and/or adoption of the program has reached nearly a saturation level of meeting statewide needs.

This extensive project clearly indicates that articulated efforts between industry and education can produce a mutually acceptable program design which better prepares students for gainful employment and job advancement.

Professional Association   California Business Education Association, through its Long-Range Planning Committee, again served as a sounding board for the needs of business educators. The Chancellor's office staff worked closely with this Long-Range Planning Committee to better meet emerging teacher and student needs in both office and distributive education.

Business Education Management Conferences   The Chancellor's Office, Occupational Division, continued participation in the design and operation of the Business Education Management Conferences. As in previous years, a northern and southern setting were conference sites, with representatives from 50 California Community Colleges in attendance.

Content for Community College participants centered around:

Planning sessions relating to business education program management, with emphasis on new concepts and trends in curriculum design, operation, and evaluation.

Vocational Education Act allocation systems, with special consideration for programs for disadvantaged and handicapped and implications for business education program management.

Accounting Teacher Workshops   Two major teacher-oriented accounting workshops were held by and for Community College accounting teachers. Fullerton Community College served as host college for the Southern California workshop, and 49 instructors attended from 21 Community Colleges. A similar accounting workshop was hosted by DeAnza College for Northern California, and 59 instructors attended from 38 Community Colleges.

The workshop program included:

Accounting enrollment attrition
Innovative teaching techniques
The two-year A.A. degree curriculum
Computer sciences and the accounting course of study
Articulation with the four-year colleges

The workshops, in addition to being well attended and thought stimulating, clearly identified an urgent need for such workshops by program areas.

Health Occupations Education

The Health Occupations programs in the 94 California Community Colleges cover 30 separate occupations. This has increased from 22 in 1969. Programs are mainly day programs and the enrollees include postsecondary and adult students.

Five Dental Assisting programs out of a total of 33 offer Extended Day education for working dental assistants. One Dental Hygiene program out of the 8 offers Extended Day education. Three of the 6 Dental Laboratory Technician programs offer Extended Day education to practitioners.

The majority of the 20 Inhalation Therapy programs offer Extended Day education to upgrade persons at the aide level. Out of 37 Medical Assisting programs, 7 offer Extended Day education.

The Nursing divisions in 54 colleges offer continuing education on a demand basis for improvement of current practice. All of the Associate Degree and Vocational Nursing programs make provision for upward articulation. The 25 Radiologic Technician programs offer Extended Day education upon demand from licensed practitioners and medical persons requiring Radiologic Safety education

There has been an appreciable increase in numbers of programs in the following health occupations since 1969:

PROGRAM	1969	1971
Dental Assisting	28	33
Dental Hygiene	3	8
Inhalation Therapy	3	20
Medical Assisting	21	37
Associate Degree Nursing (R.N.)	44	54
Vocational Nursing	56	63
Radiologic Technician	13	25
Emergency Medical Technician	0	6
Psychiatric Technician	0	14

The other programs have remained constant and in some cases have been curtailed due to the studied needs of the local communities through the efforts of the local advisory groups and educational committees.

There is a total of 320 program offerings in Health Occupational programs in the 94 California Community Colleges.

Enrollments:

There were 5,803 full-time students enrolled in the two-year Associate Degree R.N. program in 54 colleges in June, 1972, and 1,902 graduated from these programs.

There were approximately 5,100 full-time Vocational Nursing students enrolled in October, 1971, and approximately 4,080 graduated in July, 1972.

Core curriculums are being tried in the allied health clusters at the majority of the California Community Colleges. None has been completely satisfactory at this time, but a foundation program for health science is emerging.

The transitional program in Dental Assisting at Pasadena City College is still in progress, but has only a limited number of high school students who desire to meet the rigorous discipline of this type of program.

Compton College is continuing its readiness program for nursing for summer high school enrollees.

Consumer and Homemaking Education

Each year increased interest in the need for and development of Consumer and Homemaking Education programs is expressed by districts. During 1971-72, three new districts were added to the growing list of Community College districts participating under this program.

During the 1971–72 year, Community Colleges with Part F—Consumer and Homemaking Education—programs participated in two projects on Educational Accountability. Each project was a first-of-its-kind.

Consumer and Homemaking Education has been represented in the consortium of Community Colleges, cooperating with the Chancellor's Office on a special evaluation project for occupational education. The project titled "Selection and Orientation of Teams for Implementing and Refining Procedures for Evaluation of Occupational Education" was initiated in the fall of 1971. Three persons with consumer and homemaking experience were instrumental in the design and field testing of an evaluation system which has become known as COPES, Community College Program Evaluation System. The COPES system is applicable to consumer and homemaking education, and in one major field test COPES was applied to a Consumer and Homemaking Program at Bakersfield College. COPES' function is to help a college assess *what is* in relation to *what is desirable* in occupational education, in this instance consumer and homemaking education.

The second evaluation project was conducted by Tadlock Associates, Inc. This is one of the first statewide efforts in California to assess the status and effectiveness of the hoped for changes in Consumer and Homemaking Education in the high school and Community College level.

In order to asses the impact of these programs at the Community College level between 1969 and 1972, six Community College districts were selected by random sample. The six Community Colleges were dispersed throughout the state. Two of the colleges selected were rural in nature, one was urban, and three were suburban. One college has a large Mexican-American population within its service area and two others have significant Black populations within their service areas. All six colleges had developed special community outreach programs in economically depressed areas or areas with high rates of unemployment, using all or part of federal funds.

A Pilot Television Production Workshop for Home Economics was held at Fullerton Junior College, where instructors were afforded the opportunity to get acquainted with television equipment and techniques and to develop short telelessons for classroom use.

Home Economics Occupational Education

The Community Colleges continued to play a major role in responding to the demands for the preparation of well-trained individuals to be employed in a variety of early childhood education programs. A total of 58 Community Colleges offered programs related to early childhood development.

Technical Education

Technical Education enrollments were 50,443, an increase of 10,551, or 7.9 percent, over the previous year.

Although specific employment opportunities for graduates of environmental technology programs are difficult to identify, interest in implementing programs remains high. Several local studies have been completed which analyzed opportunities. Recommendations from these studies will provide information upon which to base program implementation and curricula.

Changing processes, equipment, and materials utilized in manufacturing resulting in changes in training requirements prompted writing of the curriculum guide, *Manufacturing Technology in California Community Colleges*. The publication was partially financed by the Society of Manufacturing Engineers and was presented at their annual meeting. The guide has received national interest.

Through a federal grant from the National Institute for Occupational Safety and Health, a statewide survey of need for occupational safety and health technicians was conducted. In addition, the grant financed the development of a suggested two-year postsecondary curriculum. Survey results and the curriculum are in the publication, *Curriculum Guide for Occupational Safety and Health Technicians*. Several Community Colleges are expected to implement the program in the near future.

With an increasing number of advanced technical training opportunities available, articulation efforts have had to be increased. Results are a better understanding of educational requirements resulting in little or no loss of students' work and credit if they decide to take advanced training.

Trade and Industrial Education

Trade and Industrial Education enrollments in the Community Colleges were 163,174, an increase of 52,770, or 6.8 percent, over last year.

The *State of California Plan for Equal Opportunity in Apprenticeship* went into effect in 1971–72. This plan mandates that Joint Apprenticeship Committees (JAC's) will bring into their programs a ratio of minority apprentices that is in keeping with the ratios of such minorities in the area of jurisdiction of the JAC. The period for full compliance is the period of apprenticeship in the different trades. Community Colleges submit an annual ethnic report to the Chancellor's Office showing the enrollment of minorities in the different apprenticeship programs.

The acquisition of Federal Excess Property by many Community Colleges has greatly increased training opportunities, particularly in Trade and Industrial Education. Equipment, supplies, and materials acquired allowed districts to extend purchases to better serve students.

Individualized and self-paced instruction is being instituted in many program areas of industrial education. Several colleges have developed multimedia individualized packages and utilize an open-entrance, open-exit teaching method. To facilitate development, colleges in several areas of the state have organized consortiums. Packages are exchanged freely among members and are sold for minimal costs to colleges outside the group.

Public Service Education

Current enrollment in Public Service programs is 20,886, an increase of 51 percent over last year. The most significant increase was in Government Supervision and Mangement programs, with a 462 percent jump. Other programs with a sizable increase in enrollment were Instructional Associate, 55 percent and Instructional Media Technician, 60 percent. New programs added to the list are Gerontology and Therapeutic Recreation Activity Leader.

A program of 80 slides with a synchronized tape was developed for recruitment to Library Technical Assistant programs. Curriculum guides, *Social Services: A Suggested Associate Degree Curriculum; Recreation Leadership;* and *Instructional Associate: Guidelines and Course Content for Community Colleges,* were distributed.

Through a statewide advisory committee, an articulation agreement that allows a student to go from the associate degree Social Services program to Schools of Social Work Education at four-year colleges was developed. The California Society of Parks and Recreation and the Chancellor's Office sponsored an articulation agreement recognizing the Recreation Leadership program as the foundation for a four-year Recreation major.

Criminal Justice Education

The Criminal Justice Education program in the Community Colleges was located on 74 campuses and had an enrollment of 25,485 students, an increase of 9.4 percent over the previous year.

The Chancellor's Office, California Community Colleges, together with the California Association of Administration of Justice Educators, developed and published basic outlines for a new five-course core curriculum in criminal justice education. Three new criminal justice manuals were delivered to the Chancellor's Office. They were developed by individual Community Colleges on a project basis.

Fifteen instructor training programs were conducted for criminal justice personnel in cooperation with the University of California at Los Angeles; 450 instructors completed this program. Distribution of an estimated 13,100 instructional manuals on criminal justice was accomplished through the cooperation of the Documents Section, Department of General Services.

EVALUATION PROJECT FOR POSTSECONDARY
VOCATIONAL EDUCATION

In the fall of 1971, a special grant project titled "Selection and Orientation of Teams for Implementing and Refining Procedures for Evaluation of Occupational Education Programs" was initiated.

The project objective, "... to select and orient six, three-man teams and to utilize them in the process of refining and standardizing on-site evaluation practices for occupational programs in the California Community Colleges," was achieved by June, 1972. The total number of persons so oriented was actually twenty-two. The project is now better known throughout the California Community Colleges by the acronym "COPES," Community College Occupational Program Evaluation System.

In the process of achieving the above objective, two documents utilized in developing and refining the on-site evaluation process, "COPES Guide" and "COPES Guide-Instrumentation," were produced. In addition to "refining and standardizing a practice," these documents outline a *system* for evaluating occupational education in the California Community Colleges.

COPES is a cooperative research and development project between approximately twenty California Community Colleges and the Chancellor's Office in Sacramento.

SELECTED DATA ON
POSTSECONDARY VOCATIONAL EDUCATION PROGRAMS IN
CALIFORNIA DURING FISCAL YEAR 1971–72

Program	Number of Programs	Enroll- ments	Percent Total of post- secondary Enroll- ment	Percent of Total Day Spent in Program	Number of Program Comple- tions
Agricultural Education	205	12,846	1.6	60	2,929
Distributive Education	190	55,811	6.5	40	9,344
Health Occupations Education	320	29,582	3.5	82	10,083
Home Economics Occupational Education	88	42,953	5.0	25	2,517
Office Education	352	184,555	21.7	68	47,121
Technical Education	160	50,443	5.9	75	10,316
Trade and Industry	684	163,174	19.1	75	29,220
Total	1,999	539,359	63.3	--	111,530

NOTE: Figures in this table are based on enrollments reported to the Chancellor's Office for 1970–71 and increased by an estimated 5 percent for 1971–72. Program completions based upon reports for 1970–71 with an estimated increase of 2.5 percent for 1971–72.